OECD Studies on Water

AF695106

Improving Domestic Financial Support Mechanisms in Moldova's Water and Sanitation Sector

OECD

BETTER POLICIES FOR BETTER LIVES

This work is published under the responsibility of the Secretary-General of the OECD. The opinions expressed and arguments employed herein do not necessarily reflect the official views of OECD member countries.

This document and any map included herein are without prejudice to the status of or sovereignty over any territory, to the delimitation of international frontiers and boundaries and to the name of any territory, city or area.

Please cite this publication as:
OECD (2017), *Improving Domestic Financial Support Mechanisms in Moldova's Water and Sanitation Sector*, OECD Studies on Water, OECD Publishing, Paris.
http://dx.doi.org/10.1787/9789264252202-en

ISBN 978-92-64-25219-6 (print)
ISBN 978-92-64-25220-2 (PDF)

Series: OECD Studies on Water
ISSN 2224-5073 (print)
ISSN 2224-5081 (online)

Photo credits: Cover © Taro Yamada/Corbis; © Valentin Bordeniuc.

Corrigenda to OECD publications may be found on line at: *www.oecd.org/about/publishing/corrigenda.htm*.

Foreword

This project was undertaken by the OECD with the financial support of the European Union, which is gratefully acknowledged.

Objectives

This project was aimed at streamlining and strengthening the mechanisms that channel domestic financial support to water supply and sanitation in Moldova. It has done so by mapping and reviewing existing mechanisms and by recommending adjustments, based on thorough analysis and good international practice.

Project overview

This report has been prepared as a contribution to the National Policy Dialogue (NPD) on Water Policy in Moldova conducted in co-operation with the European Union Water Initiative (EUWI) and facilitated by the OECD GREEN Action Programme Task Force (former EAP Task Force) and the United Nations Economic Commission for Europe (UNECE).

The project had four stages:

Stage 1: inventory of mechanisms that channel domestic financial support to water supply and sanitation in Moldova

Stage 2: review of selected existing mechanisms

Stage 3: search for alternatives

Stage 4: prepare draft recommendations.

In the Moldovan policy context, the following main processes and frameworks have been important for the project:

- association agreement with EU, EU Water Framework Directive (WFD) and other water-related EC Directives
- the National Environmental Strategy and the Water Supply and Sanitation (WSS) Sector Strategy for 2014-28;
- SDG6 and the policy goal of "*Water for All*"
- National Policy Dialogue under the EU Water Initiative (EUWI).

Report structure

The structure of this report is as follows:

Chapter 1 briefly presents the socio-economic context and recent trends in WSS in Moldova; it concludes on the need for stronger domestic financial support mechanisms for WSS in Moldova, including for addressing social aspects, and outlines the methodology applied in this report.

Chapter 2 presents data on financial flows in the WSS in Moldova; it focuses on own sources (user charge revenues) and external support to the sector from international development partners.

Chapter 3 presents data on financial flows that represent domestic support to the WSS sector in Moldova on the supply and demand side, i.e. to WSS systems and operators on one hand, and to customers on the other hand.

Chapter 4 presents social support systems in Moldova related to WSS (direct and indirect support, on the supply and demand side) and assesses them.

Chapter 5 contrasts the social support systems in Moldova to those of the selected reference countries. This provides the context for the assessment of the domestic financial and social support systems.

Chapter 6 formulates scenarios for the development and optimisation of WSS-related domestic financial mechanisms and social support systems. It is based on the Moldovan experience, as well as those in the reference countries.

Chapter 7 presents a short summary of key findings and conclusions of the report, as well as key recommendations. It was drafted to serve (and *de facto* was used) as a stand-alone short policy summary to be circulated and discussed with key local stakeholders in the framework of the National Policy Dialogue on water policy in Moldova.

The interim report containing Chapters 1-5 of this report was shared with stakeholders to communicate findings, verify facts and preliminary conclusions, and provide a basis for developing scenarios and recommendations. Their feedback has informed the project and this report. After the discussion at the NPD Steering Committee meeting in Chisinau on 20 May, 2015, this report was finalised.

The principal authors of the report are Suren Poghosyan of Alpha Plus Consulting and Giel Verbeeck of Treevelop with inputs from Mr Iuri Tronza and Ms Eugenia Veverita, national experts. The authors are grateful for great contributions and useful ideas from Mr Alexander Martoussevitch (OECD GREEN Action Programme Task Force) who managed this project, Ms Serafima Tronza (Ministry of Environment), and other participants of the 20th and 21st meetings of the EU Water Initiative National Policy Dialogue on Water Policy in Moldova. The authors are also grateful to Mr Krzysztof Michalak and others from OECD for their useful comments; as well as Mr Mark Foss, copy-editor, Mr Peter Vogelpoel, typesetter, and Ms Maria Dubois (OECD) for their valuable contribution in preparing the publication of the report.

The analysis, statements and any eventual errors and material omissions are, however, solely the responsibility of the authors.

The views presented in this report are those of the authors and can in no way be taken to reflect the official opinion of the government of Moldova, the European Union (EU), the OECD or of the governments of the EU and OECD member countries.

Table of contents

Figures

Tables

Boxes

Abbreviations and acronyms

ADA	Austrian Development Agency
ANRE	National Agency for Regulation in Energy
AST	Advanced Social Technologies
BNS	National Bureau of Statistics
BOOST	BOOST (data tool developed at the World Bank)
CALM	Congress of Local Authorities in Moldova
CBO	Community-Based Organisation
CMIF	Compulsory Medical Insurance Funds
DFSM	Domestic financial support mechanism(s)
EAP	Environmental Action Programme
EBRD	European Bank for Reconstruction and Development
EEA	European Environment Agency
EECCA	Eastern Europe, Caucasus and Central Asia
EIB	European Investment Bank
EUWI	European Union Water Initiative
GDN	Global Development Network
GDP	Gross Domestic Product
GDP PPP	GDP Purchasing Power Parity
GIZ	*Deutsche Gesellschaft für Internationale Zusammenarbeit*
GNI	Gross National Income
IBNET	International Benchmarking Network for Water and Sanitation Utilities
IFC	International Finance Corporation
IFRS	International Financial Reporting Standards
IMF	International Monetary Fund
lcd	Litres per capita per day
LPA	Local Public Administration
MDGs	Millennium Development Goals
MDL	Moldovan Lei

MOE	Ministry of Environment
MOF	Ministry of Finance
MRDC	Ministry of Regional Development and Construction
MTBF	Medium-term Budget Framework
NEF	National Environmental Fund
NFRD	National Fund for Regional Development
NPD	National Policy Dialogue
NRW	Non-revenue water
NSRD	National Strategy for Regional Development
OECD	Organisation for Economic Co-operation and Development
O&M	Operation and Maintenance
PFM	Public Financial Management
PIU	Project Implementation Unit
PPP	Public-private partnership
SDG	Sustainable Development Goal
SEAM	Solidarity Water Europe in Moldova
SEE	South-East Europe
SPSP	Sector Policy Support Programme for WSS in Moldova (EU-funded)
SSIB	State Social Insurance Budget
UNICEF	United Nations Children's Fund
USD	US dollar
VAT	Value Added Tax
WDI	World Development Indicators
WFD	Water Framework Directives
WHO	World Health Organization
WSS	Water Supply and Sanitation

Exchange rates (as of 30 November 2014): EUR 1 = MDL 18.7; (as of 30 April 2015): EUR 1 = MDL 20.3

Executive summary

Due to poor financial status and insufficient capital investment, the water supply and sanitation (WSS) sector in Moldova is operating beyond its optimum level. To compensate for the lack of domestic financing, development partners have invested significantly in the sector over the past 20 years. However, Moldova cannot rely upon external support indefinitely. The country must increase domestic investment and spending in the sector to meet ambitious national targets for expanding WSS infrastructure and improving service quality, while keeping services accessible and affordable, not least for the poor.

Other countries have faced similar challenges. What can the experience of reference countries selected for this study – Armenia, France, Romania and Ukraine – offer to Moldova? Is it possible to strengthen the efficiency and effectiveness of support to the sector, while safeguarding access to services for vulnerable social groups? Drawing on international experience, this report proposes options for improving and strengthening domestic financial support mechanisms for WSS in Moldova.

Key findings

- In Moldova, the most pressing mid-term challenges are to meet the requirements of the national WSS strategy and European Union Directives for environment and water; improve coverage and extend networks, especially in rural areas, to achieve the "*Water for All*" and SDG-6 policy objectives.
- Moldova implements reforms towards a more efficient and sustainable WSS, but so far key challenges have not been adequately addressed. Particularly crucial is the challenge of financial sustainability of operators while ensuring affordability of WSS services, especially for vulnerable households. In general, service delivery still suffers from lack of co-ordinated and effective planning, lack of appropriate economic regulatory system and ineffective support mechanisms.
- No single body is responsible for the entire sector, leading to fragmented approaches to planning, investment, financial flows and social support policies. Improving co-ordination between the main state actors remains a key challenge. They are the Ministry of Environment (MOE), the water agency *Apele Moldovei* and the National Environmental Fund (NEF) under the MOE; and the Ministry of Regional Development and Construction (MRDC), which manages the National Fund for Regional Development (NFRD).
- Apart from financial support from development partners, the sector receives about 2% of consolidated public funds from the state and districts (*rayons*). Both the national and municipal governments subsidise the sector, either directly or indirectly, as tariffs do not cover operation and maintenance costs, let alone allow for investment.

- The recent adoption of a universal tariff methodology aimed at full cost recovery can help improve sustainability of operators if supported by a strong social support system. But outcomes of the new methodology are yet to be seen.
- Affordability of WSS services varies greatly across the country due to high variation in local tariffs; uneven distribution of income both between regions and among rural and urban areas; and different consumption patterns.
- The poorest 20% of households receive little support to connect to WSS systems and pay WSS bills. Moreover, direct social support is not consistent across the country, failing to meet the needs of vulnerable populations. Businesses cross-subsidise vulnerable households through tariffs and this is one of the biggest social support instruments, yet providing the least value for money. Subsidies for operators of WSS systems are also inefficient, consuming resources that could be targeted towards more effective social support mechanisms. Capital expenditure subsidies and WSS-related income support deliver much greater value for money, but they are relatively small.
- Social support policy makes WSS services more affordable for vulnerable households and should be strengthened, but it cannot make these services more safe and accessible. International practice suggests more comprehensive approaches are needed to balance supply- and demand-side financial support mechanisms.
- The reference countries offer several models of water sector financing and support with three common features: more or less centralised forms of social measures using various financial support mechanisms; focus on cost recovery; and a degree of commitment to SMART policy interventions (Specific, Measurable, Attainable, Relevant, Time-bound).

Key recommendations

- Improve sector co-ordination, planning, budgeting and regulatory systems
  - *Address sector fragmentation through better co-ordination between the key actors.*
  - *Improve regional development planning, budgeting, monitoring and evaluation systems, and introduce performance-based contacts with operators.* Streamline planning, budgeting and accountability, aggregate project information and then discuss it at the sector level. Enhanced planning and budgeting will allow top-down policy directions and bottom-up funding requirements to meet in the middle. At the same time, standardising templates and information requirements (including improved performance-based systems) will ease project identification and appraisal. Comparable project databases will also simplify reporting requirements to donors. Templates developed by the OECD under an earlier project in Moldova on a mid-term action and investment plan for WSS could serve as a model.
  - *Modernise WSS infrastructure design and construction standards.* Incorporating the country's new economic and demographic realities and new water consumption patterns into these standards will allow Moldova to reduce unit costs in WSS compared to costs imposed by outdated Soviet-era norms. Relevant public and expert organisations should co-operate to find solutions to these issues.

- Enhance the nature and scope of domestic financial support mechanisms
  - *Consider the merits of four possible scenarios:* A) business as usual (BaU); B) all cards on water supply; C) framework for decentralised financial support and social measures; and D) centralised WSS financial support and social measures.

Conclusions

Selection of the preferred scenario is far from easy. Scenario A (BaU) is not recommended as it would only contribute to sustaining poverty and make the sector more vulnerable to key risks. Leaving social support to local governments (Scenario C) will arguably not yield much benefit to those who need it most. On the other hand, present conditions for a centralised approach (Scenario D) to social measures are not that favourable. However, assuming that Moldova can address the implementation risks and uncertainty of Scenario D, this scenario would presumably deliver better outcomes than Scenarios B and C. But if the assumption does not hold, Scenario B could be a preferred option.

Chapter 1

Socio-economic context, sector trends and methodology

This chapter briefly presents the socio-economic context and recent trends in water supply and sanitation (WSS) in Moldova; it concludes on the need for stronger domestic financial support mechanisms for WSS in Moldova, including for addressing social aspects, and outlines the methodology applied in this report.

1.1. Socio-economic context

General outline of Moldova's economy

Like many other countries in transition, Moldova faces significant institutional, demographic and social challenges. Substantial changes in the gross domestic product (GDP) structure have been recorded in the post-Soviet era. For instance, the share of industry has decreased from 40% to 20% in 20 years. The agriculture sector has also significantly decreased its share of GDP, even from 1999 to 2012. While the share of services in the GDP has increased from one-quarter in 1989 to almost two-thirds in 2012. Although the increasing importance of services partly reflects industrial decline, the economy of Moldova is gradually improving its performance, as indicated in Figure 1.1. Per capita data show a pattern of stable increases and the annual growth rate has been positive since 2000 (with the exception of 2009 due to the economic crisis).

Figure 1.1. **Economic performance of Moldova in 1990-2013**

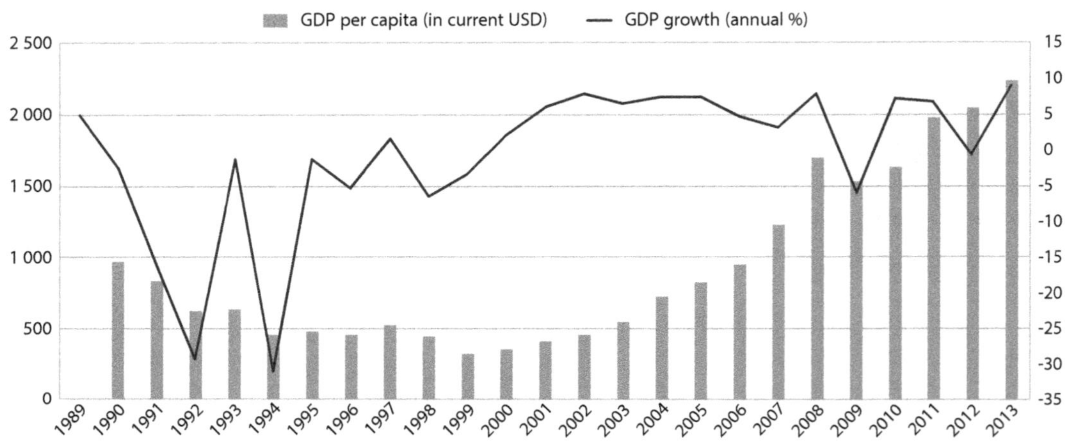

Source: WDI database, World Bank, http://databank.worldbank.org/data/reports.aspx?source=world-development-indicators.

A main macroeconomic concern is inflation, which only recently went below 5%. Policy analysis by the International Monetary Fund and World Bank shows concern about weak governance in the banking sector, eroded fiscal discipline and lack of structural reforms. The depreciation of the Moldovan Lei (MDL) by 20% between November 2014 and April 2015 was another major concern.

As Table 1.1 illustrates, Moldova has remained among the poorest countries in Europe.

Table 1.1. **Per capita income in selected countries in Balkans and the EECCA region, 2012 data**

Country	GNI	GDP	GDP PPP	GNI PPP
Moldova	2 070	2 037	3 424	3 690
Georgia	3 280	3 542	5 902	5 860
Ukraine	3 500	3 877	7 418	7 290
Kosovo	3 640	n.a.	2 300	n.a.
Armenia	3 720	2 990	6 645	6 990

Note: **GNI**: gross national income; **PPP**: purchasing power parity ; **n.a.**: data not available.

Source: World Bank for GNI per capita in 2012 (nominal), Atlas method, WDI database, World Bank, http://databank.worldbank.org/data/reports.aspx?source=world-development-indicators.

As Table 1.2. indicates, remittances from Moldovans living or working abroad add between 25-33% to the GDP. Of all the reference countries, only Armenia comes close to this figure. Clearly, the large amount of remittances partly mitigates the effect of low per capita GDP.

Table 1.2. **Estimated size of remittances as percentage of GDP**

Country	2010	2011	2012	2013
Moldova	23	22	24	25
Armenia	18	18	19	21
Macedonia, FYR	4	4	4	4
Romania	2	2	2	2
Ukraine	5	5	5	5
France	1	1	1	1

Source: WDI database, World Bank, http://databank.worldbank.org/data/reports.aspx?source=world-development-indicators.

Being a small open economy highly dependent on remittances, Moldova is subject to various external shocks; a series of trade, energy and other shocks has already affected the economy. Inter alia, the economic and financial crisis in the Russian Federation has negatively affected the level of remittances to Moldova, especially since the last two months of 2014.

In a National Bureau of Statistics (2014) report, about 71% of the total number of households assessed their living standard as satisfactory; another 10% estimated their living conditions as good or very good. Around 20% of the population believed they live below accepted living standards. Only 5.5% of respondents believed they lived better in the year the survey took place than in the previous year, while 30% believed the situation had worsened.

Poverty headcount

Income per capita in Moldova is the lowest in Europe. Consequently, given the distribution of income and the absolute low levels of income, a large number of people live below the poverty line (see Table 1.3).

This dynamic is reflected in the affordability of WSS services in the country. The national WSS Strategy for 2014-28 indicates a significant portion of the Moldovan population is paying more than 5% of their household income for WSS services (see Figure 1.2); this is the threshold typically applied by international institutions to low-income developing countries. Therefore, these households are exposed to water affordability risk and may experience problems with paying their WSS bills.

Table 1.3. **Percentage of people living below the national poverty line in selected countries**

Country	World Bank	Year	CIA	Year
Ukraine	2.9	2008	35.0	2009
Belarus	5.4	2009	27.1	2003 est.
Latvia	5.9	2004	n.a.	n.a.
Montenegro	6.6	2010	6.6	2010 est.
Poland	7.6	2008	10.2	2003 est.
Kazakhstan	8.2	2009	8.2	2009
Serbia	9.2	2010	8.8	2010 est.
Bulgaria	10.6	2007	21.8	2008
Croatia	11.1	2004	18.0	2009
Russian Federation	11.1	2006	13.1	2010
Albania	12.4	2008	12.5	2008 est.
Romania	13.8	2006	21.1	2010
Bosnia and Herzegovina	14.0	2007	18.6	2007 est.
Azerbaijan	15.8	2008	6.0	2012 est.
Turkey	18.1	2009	16.9	2010
Macedonia, Republic of	19.0	2006	30.9	2010
Moldova	21.9	2010	26.3	2009
West Bank and Gaza	21.9	2009	n.a.	n.a.

Note: **est.**: estimate; **n.a.**: not available: **CIA**: United States Central Intelligence Agency.

Source: World Databank. Databank.worldbank.org (accessed 17 November 2012).

Figure 1.2. **Percentage of total household expenditure spent on WSS in Moldova, by deciles**

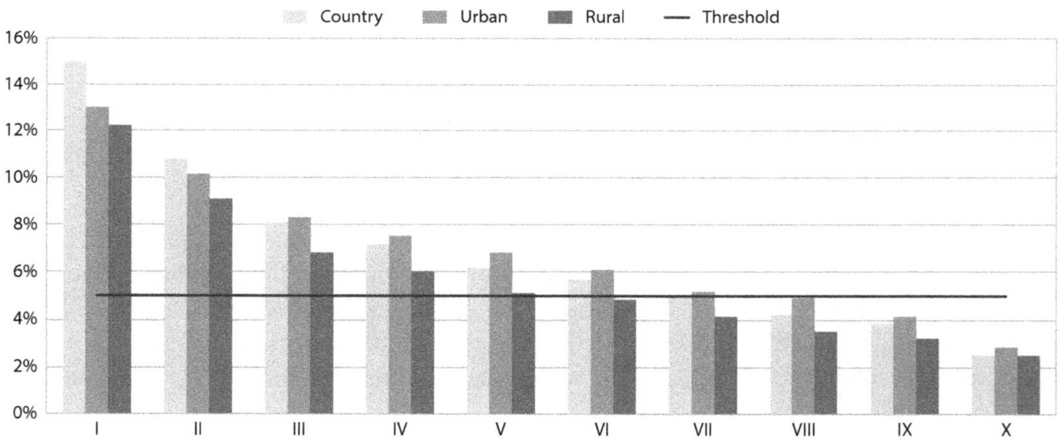

Source: Government of Moldova, WSS Strategy for 2014-18, http://lex.justice.md/ru/352311/.

1.2. Institutional framework, WSS sector trends and needs for stronger DFSM

Institutional framework

The institutional framework of the WSS sector in Moldova is presented in Table 1.4 below.

Table 1.4. **WSS sector institutional framework**

Water management		
Ministry of Environment – main actor that develops and promotes state policy in this area.		
Water Agency "Apele Moldovei" implements water management and state policies in hydrology, water and sanitation, and protection of settlements and agricultural land against flooding.	***Service providers (incl. Apacanals)*** are 21 enterprises and organisations subordinate to the "Apele Moldovei". *Associations of water consumers* manage water supply systems and water sanitation in rural areas.	***Moldova Apa-Canal Association*** provides training and technical support to its members (31 municipal enterprises and 7 joint stock companies).
National Agency for Regulation in Energy (ANRE) prepares costing methodology, and WSS tariffs approval and implementation.	***Local public administrations*** are authorised by law to commission the management, renting or leasing of local property and public services at district level.	***State Ecologic Inspectorate*** authorises special water usage and shares ecological expertise.

Source: from WSS sector expenditures strategy for 2015-17 MTBF.

The WSS in Moldova comprises 39 incorporated water utilities (Apacanals) and some 500 municipal enterprises or waterworks in rural areas. Urban operators serve 42% of the total population. The two largest cities, Chisinau and Balti, comprise half of that urban population. The remaining 37 operators serve cities with a population of 15 000 each, on average. Centralised systems in 977 villages serve rural areas. In addition, 651 hamlets have no centralised water supply system.

Local government owns water and waste water infrastructure, and transfers assets for economic management to utility operators.

The Ministry of Environment (MOE), the Ministry of Regional Development and Construction, and the Ministry of Health mainly set policy in the sector. Within MOE, the water agency Apele Moldovei implements sector policy.

Apacanals

The Apacanals are legal entities that own, manage, operate and maintain the public water and sewage systems and provide consumers with public water and sanitation services. Their activities are licensed by the National Agency for Regulation in Energy (ANRE). Fixed assets (WSS systems) are on the balance sheet of respective Apacanals. Irrespective of their organisational form, the Apacanals must ensure:

- sampling, handling, transport, storage and distribution of water and sanitation
- exploitation of public water supply and public sewerage system in compliance with the technologies and operating instructions
- monitoring of the quality of drinking water and wastewater
- maintaining the public water and sewage systems in a state of continuous operation, with the exception of *force majeure*

- improving the efficiency of public water and sewage systems to reduce costs by reducing production costs, and specific consumption of raw materials, fuel and electricity, and by retrofitting, refurbishing and modernising systems.

Association of Apacanals of Moldova was created by the Apacanals in 2000. The association supports Apacanals in improving their capacities, as well as protecting their interests in local and central public administration authorities and elsewhere.

In the past, operators proposed tariffs, which were then approved by local councils. As of mid-September 2014, ANRE has started to regulate WSS tariffs as well.

Economic Regulator (ANRE)

ANRE, which also became responsible for regulating the WSS sector only in September 2014, has the following primary responsibilities:

- licensing (on WSS service provision in a region, district, municipality or city)
  - extending, amending, suspending or withdrawing temporary licences
- establishing rules for tariff calculation and approval
  - developing and approving methodology on WSS tariffs
  - approving tariffs for public technical water service to a region, district, municipality or a city
- monitoring sectoral application of tariffs (regulation on public service quality indicators of WSS).

From this list one can see that ANRE plays a key role in determining tariff rates and hence user charge revenues of municipal water utilities (*Apacanals*) in Moldova.

Tariff regulation

Moldova revised the WSS tariffs regulation system and 2014 when the sector regulator (ANRE) received additional authorities to approve and impose WSS tariffs if and when municipalities fail to do so themselves. The approved uniform methodology for determining, approving and applying tariffs for public water supply, sewerage and wastewater treatment is based on a recently adopted legislative requirement; Article 7 of the Law 303 on public water supply and sewage system requires ANRE to develop and approve such methodology.

The methodology has been upgraded to more appropriate requirements, including on modern accounting standards. It envisages that the tariff setting must incorporate the following categories:

- tariff for water supply
- charges for the water supply service
- service charges for sewage and wastewater.

The charges may vary based on geography, households' place of consumption, type of dwelling (own apartments, individual houses, etc.) and type of contract for service delivery (one contract for the housing block or a separate contract with each apartment owner).

This methodology provides the following structure of costs that will determine the tariffs:

- costs of depreciation of tangible and intangible assets

- expenses on water obtained
- material expenses
- expenses for electricity
- staff remuneration
- costs of maintenance and operation of public water systems and sanitation
- distribution expenses
- administrative expenses
- other expenses of the operator.

An important factor related to developing methodologies referred to consistency in applying terminology and requirements set out in the new national accounting standards.

The methodology will be in force for five years, with the first-year costs becoming baselines. The tariffs will use the baselines, adjusting for inflation (measured in terms of industrial deflator) for subsequent years.

Sector trends

This study took place in an environment subject to change. In analysing problems and devising solutions, the following sector trends and observations are to be taken into account (most already play a role in Moldova):

- Political commitment to the implementation of targets and obligation set in the national strategies (National Development Strategy to 2020; National Environmental Strategy and the National WSS Strategy for 2014-28, as well as the Energy and Adaptation to Climate Change Strategies) and the Association Agreement with the EU. "*Water-for-all*" and Sustainable Development Goal (SDG) commitment drives the Moldovan WSS strategy towards continuous expansion of the WSS system to significantly increase coverage by building new infrastructure.
- Financial flows in WSS are small (see Table 2.1 for 2013 data), insufficient to ensure financial autonomy of the sector.
- An unsustainable **over-reliance on external support** (mostly EU funds) for investment in WSS. The national and local Governments need to co-finance EU-funded capital expenditure and generate the required funds from domestic sources. Hence, a rebalancing (of external and domestic sources) and strengthening domestic financial support mechanisms is needed in parallel with a well-targeted and effective social support system.
- The need to improve effectiveness and cost-effectiveness of both external and domestic support to WSS, especially in the area of WSS infrastructure development based on appropriate criteria and realistic demand assessments. This can be achieved through revising the national standards for design and construction of WSS systems.
- The need to improve operators' business models plus community-based organisation (CBO) models and make them sustainable in the context of local solidarity and mutual support mechanisms.

- Regionalisation of water supply to absorb more investment funding, pool human resources and facilities, improve service delivery and accountability, and enhance efficiency. The most outspoken example in this respect is Romanian experience.
- More and more South-East Europe (SEE) countries establishing independent economic regulators to limit tariff-setting competences of local government. Moldova has taken important steps in this direction by expanding the mandate of the ANRE with respect to regulating WSS tariffs.
- Increasing dependence of funding for investment in WSS on the willingness to charge cost-recovering tariffs and eliminate counter-productive cross-subsidies. In the case of loan or other market-based financing, charges simply have to increase to service the debt. However, grant-financed investments come with conditions on the operators' financial self-sustainability.
- The need for governments to apply economic instruments for environmental and water policies. Since some of these instruments will affect the WSS bill, governments need to co-finance EU-funded capital expenditure and generate the required funds from domestic sources. Environmental charges on abstraction and pollution are one of the possibilities that will directly or indirectly affect the costs of WSS services.

To address the sector's challenges, regionalisation of services is foreseen, but there is no firm central policy to guide this transition. A handful of regionalisation projects exist, sometimes funded from domestic sources through the National Fund for Regional Development (NFRD) and sometimes paid for by the international financial institutions (IFIs) or development agencies. According to World Bank (2013), most regionalisation efforts are initiated without central co-ordination and a clear contractual model.

1.3. Rationale

In general, the water supply and sanitation sector in Moldova is not financially sustainable; tariffs typically do not cover even full operational costs. WSS sector development requires a targeted policy for ensuring the financial sustainability of operators complemented by targeted support of those domestic users of WSS services in need (demand-side support measures). However, due to widespread poverty and tough affordability constraints, full financial autonomy and self-sufficiency of the WSS sector cannot be achieved in the mid-term. The sector will require financial support from the public sector and donors probably for a couple of decades to come.

On the supply side, capital investments are funded mostly from the central public budget or by development partners – the external partners fund capital investments either through the public financial system or directly for some specific projects in the municipalities.

External support to capital investments in WSS is substantial, but Moldova cannot rely on a permanent donor support in the long-term. As a result, domestic financial support mechanisms (DFSMs) will have to play a significant role in WSS over the next few decades and the effectiveness of DFSMs must be enhanced. Indeed, the previous OECD work on mid-term Action and Investment plan for WSS highlighted that existing DFSMs often operated in a non-co-ordinated way, or provided support to projects that are local priority but not always the national priority.[1]

This challenged was realised by the Ministry of Environment and it asked OECD, as facilitator of the NPD on water policy in Moldova, to help identify feasible options for streamlining and strengthening domestic financial support mechanisms through which support to the WSS sector could and should be provided. This study addressed the demand from the key local stakeholders leading the NPD.

1.4. Methodology

Definition of DFSM

The definition of DFSM used in this report is provided in Box 1.1

Box 1.1. **Domestic financial support mechanisms**

In this report, **domestic financial support mechanisms (DFSMs)** in WSS are defined as a combination of financial support to owners and operators of WSS systems, and to end-users of WSS services from the state and local (municipal, community) budgets, including loans but excluding grants from external donors channelled via the national public finance management (PFM) system; and support to some consumer groups provided by other groups via tariffs (cross-subsidies) or from local charity and mutual support funds. The support might be provided in the form of cash transfers, cross-subsidies, public revenues or water utility revenues foregone.

On the supply side, the government of Moldova has several DFSMs for interventions in the sector, although it is largely using in-budget funds to support investments in WSS. Municipalities are the main owners of the water supply companies (operators) and provide them with direct or indirect support. Given the various instruments in use, there is increasing need to harmonise public financial management policy.

On the demand side, cross-subsidies prevail. Social support mechanisms are not sufficiently developed, despite significant poverty levels in the country. This reduces the flexibility of decisions over the tariff policy when the economic regulator and the municipalities want to increase tariffs to cover the costs and help operators achieve financial sustainability.

Several factors can influence the relative priority in finding the optimal combination of the two-sided support mechanisms, including time horizon, impact of economic cycles and external shocks. For instance, extensive supply-side efforts may be more adequate at times of rapid economic growth. Demand-side support may be more relevant when growth is slowed down and targeted social support becomes more a priority.

Source : Based on authors' findings.

Method

The study has made use of contributions from both national and international experts. First, it describes and analyses the existing situation with DFSMs. Building on the analysis, it formulates scenarios to guide thinking and inform decisions about possible improvements, and to develop recommendations.

Sources of data and information

Various sources informed the inventory of the DFSMs:

- Official data from the Ministry of Finance were useful in identifying the scope and nature of the state budget support mechanisms, presented in Chapter 3.

- State budget, Medium-term Budget Framework (MTBF) and the BOOST database (a multi-year database of state and rayon budgets) were the primary source of data for the analysis of financial support mechanisms (in terms of cash flow).
- Data on the performance of the two national funds (NFRD and NEF) most relevant for WSS were analysed using official data from the Ministry of Environment and the Ministry of Regional Development and Construction on project identification and appraisal processes.
- A small-scale survey (not representative of the country) of WSS operators and other stakeholders identified the country's major financial support mechanisms in WSS. The 12 main operators provided solid information on main cash flow items in the sector, and social support and social responsibility measures, as well as explicit and implicit subsidy channels and scales.

Quantitative analysis was based on a survey among relevant stakeholders in the sector and IBNET, WDI and BOOST databases. IBNET was used for analysing the performance of the water sector in Moldova, but also to allow for a comparison with the selected reference countries. BOOST was used in assessing the public (state and municipal) financial flows in the sector. State budget data, Ministry of Finance documents, sector strategies and other reference documents on the WSS sector were useful in assessing the sector specific data and putting them into the context.

Selection of reference countries

Chapter 5 was developed through desk study of current practices in selected reference countries that employ both supply- and demand-side financial and social support mechanisms in WSS.

The reference countries have been selected on the basis of the following:

Armenia is also a small state of the former Soviet Union. In its economic and geopolitical orientation, Armenia falls between the Russian Federation and the EU. With its GDP 50% above that of Moldova, Armenia is markedly wealthier, but more comparable to Moldova than most EU countries. Reform in the water sector has also proceeded further, although it remains strongly dependent on state subsidies and investment funding. Armenia's social security system focused on general income support (based on a proxy for means testing) is more advanced than that of Moldova; this is an important consideration when discussing options for improving WSS-related social support measures in Moldova.

France is a developed Western European EU Member State with particularly strong water-sector finance and a long-lasting experience of private sector participation (PSP) and inter-municipal co-operation. The approach to finance and practice of a welfare state with respect to WSS-related social measures and solidarity mechanisms is of big interest to key stakeholders in Moldova.

Romania is quite similar to Moldova in terms of language and culture, as well as socio-economic aspects. Moreover, it is a new EU Member State, which is Moldova's aspiration. Romania has also proceeded on a similar development curve. Experience obtained in Romania is valuable for Moldova.

Ukraine also shares history with Moldova as part of the former Soviet Union. Although its GDP per capita is almost double that of Moldova, the institutional development of its water sector has a comparable structure. Of particular interest is Ukraine's housing subsidies system, which takes WSS charges into account. It is the only reference country that operates a burden limitation system. The country's experience is therefore of relevance to Moldova.

Assessment of various support mechanisms

Responses from the 12 Apacanals and other stakeholders allowed assessment of expectations and perceptions of those organisations over the current and possible social support mechanisms; these aspects are reflected in social support systems in Moldova related to WSS described in Chapter 4. Main categories of such support were related to increasing the connection rates to WSS systems, tariff-related measures and income support measures. The package covers the supply- and demand-side measures. It reflects the current needs in the development of the WSS sector in Moldova with an aim to balance the financial and social costs of reforms. The project team analysed various domestic financial support mechanisms under each category with an assessment and comparison of their effectiveness and efficiency. The assessment results were presented for discussion.

Note

1. The 2011 OECD report *Supporting the Development of a Mid-Term Action and Investment Plan for WSS in Moldova* was submitted as a PDF document to the Ministry of Environment of Moldova. More details on the output documents are available upon request.

References

Government of Moldova (2014), *WSS Strategy for 2014-28*, http://lex.justice.md/ru/352311/

NBS (2014), *Aspects of the standard of living of population in 2013, Results of the household budget survey*, National Bureau of Statistics of the Republic of Moldova, Chisinau.

World Bank (2013), *Water sector regionalisation review, Republic of Moldova*, World Bank, Washington, DC.

World Development Indicators (WDI) database, World Bank, http://databank.worldbank.org/data/reports.aspx?source=world-development-indicators, accessed 24 September 2014.

Chapter 2

Financial performance of, and external support to, the water supply and sanitation sector in Moldova

This chapter presents data on overall financial flows in the water supply and sanitation (WSS) in Moldova; then it focuses on own sources (user charge revenues) and external support to the sector from international development partners; domestic support-related financial flows will be discussed in the next chapter.

Table 2.1 presents data on overall financial flows in the WSS sector and major sources of finance.

Table 2.1. **Indicative table on WSS financial flows in 2013**

Source of finance	2013 (in MDL thousands)	As percentage of total
Water users (user charge revenues of Apacanals)	843 074	48
Ministry of Environment	592 304	34
Donors (via national PFM system), including loans	251 278	14
Ministry of Regional Development and Construction	63 918	4
TOTAL	1 750 574	100

Source: Based on BOOST database, http://wbi.worldbank.org/boost/boost-initiative, MOF data.

One can see that external donors are the top three major sources of finance for the WSS sector in Moldova.

This chapter focuses on own sources (user charge revenues) and external support to the sector from international development partners (donors), while domestic support will be discussed in the next chapter.

2.1. User charge revenues and financial position of water utilities

User charge revenues of Apacanals

Municipal water utilities (*Apacanals*) generate the biggest portion of domestic financial flows in the WSS sector. User charges for WSS services are the main source of Apacanals' revenues. The overall financial and non-financial parameters are presented in Table 2.2. They indicate that Apacanals have significantly increased collection rates and total user charge revenues, and increased the average tariff rate for 1 m^3 by almost 1.5 times over 2009-13.

Table 2.2. **Total water sales and fees collected by Moldovan operators, 2009-13**

Indicators	Units	2009	2010	2011	2012	2013
I. Water supply, total	000 m^3	61 707.9	58 666.7	57 721.9	57 864.5	58 392.7
population	000 m^3	47 310.1	45 259.4	44 633.1	44 554.7	45 385.7
other	000 m^3	14 422.9	13 407.3	13 088.8	13 309.8	13 007.0
Income from sales, total	000 MDL	463 673.8	573 670.5	572 617.7	605 597.8	612 371.8
population	000 MDL	267 571.5	369 168.0	369 034.1	383 794.1	399 263.6
enterprises	000 MDL	196 102.3	204 502.5	203 583.6	221 803.7	213 108.2
II. Wastewater received from subscribers	000 m^3	53 149.8	51 558.2	50 792.7	50 027.1	50 838.4
population	000 m^3	40 189.2	38 697.7	37 978.7	37 347.5	38 275.2
enterprises	000 m^3	12 960.6	12 860.5	12 814.4	12 679.6	12 563.2
III. Income from water sanitation	000 MDL	194 190.8	217 978.7	217 424.4	225 926.6	230 702.4
population	000 MDL	50 912.2	65 133.2	65 481.4	69 621.8	73 247.1
enterprises	000 MDL	143 278.6	152 845.6	151 943.0	156 305.0	157 455.0

Table 2.2. **Total water sales and fees collected by Moldovan operators, 2009-13** *(continued)*

Indicators	Units	2009	2010	2011	2012	2013
Average tariffs/costs						
Average tariff rate per 1 m³ of drinking water	MDL	6.66	8.60	8.82	9.20	9.30
Cost per 1 m³ of drinking water	MDL	7.15	7.89	8.40	8.70	9.30
Average tariff rate for sewage (per 1 m³)	MDL	2.82	4.23	4.30	4.50	4.50
Cost per 1 m³ for sewage	MDL	3.31	5.14	5.60	5.80	6.80

Source: Developed by authors based on AMAC (association "Moldova Apacanal") database, www.amac.md.

Financial position

Another important dimension for assessing the financial system of the WSS sector is the financial position (and flows) of Apacanals – the main water supply and sanitation organisations. Most of the Apacanals operating in Moldova are in public (municipal) property. This affects the financial performance of the sector, and must be taken into account in long-term policy making.

Box 2.1. **Excerpt from the Auditor's Report**

"The Company is highly geared and dependent upon the continuing financial support of its founder without which there would be significant doubt about its ability to continue as a going concern as well as its ability to realise its assets and discharge its liabilities in the ordinary course of business."

Source: Auditor's Report on one of the Apacanals (*restricted, seen in draft*).

Overall financial performance of the Apacanals indicates very poor sustainability. According to data from the survey by the project (as well as audit reports of Apacanals), most Apacanals rely on support from their shareholders (municipalities). This support may not necessarily be in the form of cash. However, the auditor's report and response to the survey (see below) indicate that the audited WSS companies generate and accumulate losses.

The project has obtained primary data on financial performance. A small group of municipal Apacanals were surveyed in the first months of the project. Responses from 12 Apacanals (see Annex C) show around MDL 100 million of annual losses in the sector (see Table 2.4). This, however, is not the whole picture, but only from the 12 main Apacanals that responded to the survey. According to financial statements of Apacanals, the sector is subsidised; many stakeholders claimed the opposite during inception phase meetings. Most of the agencies, Apacanals themselves and other stakeholders argued the WSS sector and tariffs must be (and are) commercial. However, as the reviewed audit reports indicate, the stock of subsidies (as non-current liabilities) may represent as much as 75-80% of total assets of those Apacanals (see also Box 2.1).

The WSS sector, in fact, also receives subsidies and grants even now from the state and municipalities (Table 2.3). These contributions, equivalent to around 8% of sales in addition to similar amounts from donors, may not be financially significant, but they represent subsidies nonetheless. Yet many stakeholders are not aware the sector is subsidised.

Interestingly, the share of sales to businesses (46% of total) is almost equal to the one for households. This is not surprising as the tariffs are differentiated. However, this can potentially provide policy makers with room to manoeuvre; even marginal adjustments to business tariffs will have a noticeable impact on the overall financial position. Improving collection rates for households in a cost-effective way could also influence financial performance.

Table 2.3. **Aggregate financial flows of 12 selected Apacanals**

in MDL thousands

	2013
Total sales	**748 373**
Total sales (households)	403 541
Total sales (businesses)	344 832
Collection rate, all customers	**93%**
Collection rate (households)	88%
Collection rate (businesses)	99%
Sales by subsectors	**748 373**
Sales (water supply)	542 314
Sales (water sanitation)	206 060
Grants and subsidies	**126 819**
Total grants and subsidies (water supply)	64 685
Total grants and subsidies (water sanitation)	62 134
Subsidies from Apacanals to customers	**1 440**

Source: Authors' survey of Apacanals undertaken in the framework of this project.

Table 2.4. **Aggregate financial performance of 12 selected Apacanals**

in MDL thousands

	2013
Gross profit	199 783
Other income, distribution costs, administrative expenses, finance costs and costs of other economic activities, other expenses	(290 380)
Profit before tax	(90 597)
Income tax expense	6 052
Annual profit	(96 649)

Note: (N) stands for -N (minus N, negative number).

Source: Authors' survey of Apacanals undertaken in the framework of this project.

Table 2.3 shows the biggest source of funding in the sector remains household and business customers. Despite significant cash injections from the state, municipalities and donors, sales to customers are still the main source of funding in the sector.

Such a significant financial gap, however, is not visible in countries with an outdated system of public sector accounting and where budgets reflect only cash flows of budget organisations. Modern accounting principles drawn from the International Public Sector Accounting Standards would have captured and reported information on losses and subsidies. These, in turn, would have become part of the policy agenda, including during the budget discussions (even if those do not necessarily affect budget lines).

Moldovan Apacanals produce financial statements based on International Financial Reporting Standards (IFRS), and transparently report on annual and accumulated losses. However, there is no proof this information becomes part of public finance management (PFM) and WSS-sector discussions and analytical reports. For instance, an Apacanal that had submitted financial statements has already accumulated almost MDL 8 million of losses with its Charter capital of less than MDL 10 million. The continuous policy of low tariffs vs. high unit costs may lead those companies to technical bankruptcy in a very short time.

Technical bankruptcy may not necessarily lead companies to interrupt services immediately. A company, for example, may simply have significant cash problems. However, accumulated losses signify the business has poor sustainability, which will eventually create problems such as lower quality of water supply services, increased number of failures and system malfunctions, etc.

2.2. Financial flows from donors

Donors

Co-operation with donors allows introduction of new technologies and capacities in the sector and significant investments. The government of Moldova has approved a series of policy documents at the central level to guide development of the WSS system in the country, including via donor support mechanisms. These documents are the Environmental Strategy, Strategy for Water Supply and Sanitation, Agriculture and Rural Development Strategy, Energy Strategy, the National Strategy for Regional Development, as well as water-related SDGs that replaced Millennium Development Goals (MDGs).

Donors channel project funding in various forms: directly to the local public administration (LPA), as budget support at the central level or as investment projects via Project Implementation Units (PIUs). In many cases, donors prefer direct co-operation with LPAs. This may decrease the bureaucracy of an individual project, but complicates sector policy co-ordination processes e.g. the absence of proper information on financial allocations of LPAs for specific WSS projects during the Medium-Term Budget Framework (MTBF) and budget planning. This, in turn, gets reflected in numerous cases of significant mismatches between planned budgets and actual allocations, with the latter exceeding significantly the former. Other cases may include complete absence of that information in LPA PFM systems (including on execution) in cases when donors operate through their own PIU systems.

Donors play a significant role in financing the WSS sector in Moldova, although they often use different financial systems. Table 2.5 presents grants to the sector channelled via the national budget system (and therefore, can be treated as part of the domestically operated financial mechanism). Despite the lower number of institutions providing grants, the volume of grants is impressive, both compared with the volume of loans and total volume of financial flows in the sector. The EU provides the biggest share of budgetary support for the WSS sector (in the past including through the Sector Policy Support Programme [SPSP] for WSS in Moldova).

Table 2.5. **WSS sector grants channelled via the national budget systems by donors**

in MDL thousands

	2009	2010	2011	2012	2013	2014 (plan)
European Union	250 859	159 342		181 884		132 789
GIZ, including:			1 485	2 102	69 219	13 447
Water supply and sewage system for village Duruitoarea Veche, mayoralty Costești, rayon Rîșcani					3 022	
Sewage system construction in village Duruitoarea Veche (Rîșcani)						2 189
Renovation of water treatment plant town Costeşti (Rîşcani)						5 304
Extension of sewage system in town Costeşti (Rîșcani)						5 953
Improving operational management of the Apă Canal Cahul				1 147	1 164	
Potable water supply for village Roșu			1 485	955		
Sewage system for village Roşu, rayon Cahul					12 816	
Water pipeline construction for Leova – Iargara					44 296	
Renovation of water treatment plant in Cahul					7 921	
Total	250 859	159 342	1 485	183 985	69 219	146 236

Source: Authors' own elaboration based on MOF data.

The Austrian Development Agency also provided grant funds for regional-level WSS activities. Sector grants were channelled via budget system co-funded by donors and the National Environmental Fund (e.g. Nisporeni project).

More donors are playing an active role in the WSS sector through loans than grants. Specifically, two European IFIs and two World Bank Group member institutions cover the vast majority of lending to the sector (over 95% for all years from 2009-14). Kuwait is the only bilateral donor on the list with relatively smaller lending packages available in 2009 and planned for 2014.

The level of donor support has significantly shifted from the World Bank (dominating in 2009-11) to the European IFIs (EBRD and EIB). The latter donors launched lending projects in 2011 (around half of total lending for WSS in Moldova) and then gradually increased their presence with up to 99% expected for 2014 (see Table 2.6).

Table 2.6. **WSS sector loans by donors**

in MDL thousands

	2009	2010	2011	2012	2013	2014 (plan)
World Bank	15 808.8	16 367.5	43 283.3	35 267.6	48 642.1	0.0
EBRD	0.0	0.0	1 639.7	14 672.1	69 204.9	31 216.5
EIB	0.0	0.0	0.0	15 790.2	64 212.0	31 216.5
Kuwait	777.5	0.0	0.0	0.0	0.0	133.7
IFC	0.0	56 648.0	0.0	40 770.6	0.0	0.0
Total	16 586.3	73 015.5	44 923.0	106 500.5	182 059.0	62 566.7

Source: Authors' own elaboration based on MOF data.

Various other donor projects are not part of the PFM system (budget system) of the government of Moldova. These projects vary in their nature, planning and execution systems, and are generally financed directly through the government (i.e. they do not report on cash flow to the Treasury and Ministry of Finance). While this report does not treat these projects as domestic financial mechanisms, Table 2.7 presents available data in the interests of information.

Table 2.7. **List of projects that are not part of the budget system**

Project name	Implementing agency	Beneficiary
Austrian Development Agency		
Rehabilitation of the WSS in rayon Nisporeni: mayoralties Nisporeni, Vărzăreşti and Grozeşti	Nisporeni mayor's office; Swiss Co-operation Bureau / Swiss Embassy representation in the Republic of Moldova	Mayoralties Nisporeni, Vărzăreşti, Grozeşti; Rayon Council Nisporeni; Municipal enterprise "Household water supply and sanitation", Nisporeni
Improving water management and ecosystem protection Ramsar zone "Nistrul de Jos"	S.E. BIOTICA; NGO "Rodoliubets"; NGO "Ecospectrum"; NGO "Renaşterea"	S.E. BIOTICA; NGOs "Rodoliubets", "Ecospectrum", "Renaşterea"
Consolidating capacities of providers from WSS in Republic of Moldova (AguaProf II)	AO "Institutul de Formare a Capacităţilor Profesionale" (training centre)	Ministry of Education; Ministry of Environment; VET No. 1, Bălţi; VET town Rezina; VET village Corbu; VET village Alexăndreni; Technical University continuing training centre
Promotion of good management of the water resources in south part of Moldova	AO "Centrul Naţional de Mediu"	AO "Centrul Naţional de Mediu"
Swiss Confederation – Swiss Co-operation Bureau in the Republic of Moldova (SDC) and Austrian Development Agency (ADA)		
Programme "Water and sewage system in Republic of Moldova (ApaSan)"	Swiss Co-operation Bureau representation in Republic of Moldova (SDC); ADA, SKAT, Resource and Consultation Centre for Development; Foundation Fundaţia "Moldova Branch of "SKAT" foundation, Public Society "Solidaritate, Tineri şi Apă în Moldova"	Village mayoralties from Republic of Moldova; prison for women from village Rusca; long-term care for the elderly from village Sărata-Galbenă
USAID		
Capacity building of local governments in the management of the water sector in Moldova	Congress of Local Authorities from Moldova (CALM)	Local public administrations
Rehabilitation and construction of water and sewer network to wastewater treatment plant in the town of Teleneşti	Regional Development Agency Centre (ADR Centru)	Government of Republic of Moldova; Ministry of Regional Development and Construction
European Bank for Reconstruction and Development		
Feasibility study for water supply and sewerage of Chisinau programme	SA "Apă-Canal Chişinău"; Seureca – France; SA "Business Consulting Institute"; SC Ingineria apelor SRL	SA "Apă-Canal Chişinău"

Source: Government Decision No. 246 of 8 April 2010 with all amendments, *On application of zero rate of VAT on supplies of goods, services delivered in the country*, Annex 1, *Official Monitor* 52-53, 14 April 2010.

References

Association “Moldova Apacanal” (AMAC) database, www.amac.md.

BOOST database, http://wbi.worldbank.org/boost/boost-initiative.

Government Decision No. 246 of 8 April 2010 with all amendments, *On application of zero rate of VAT on supplies of goods, services delivered in the country*, Annex 1, *Official Monitor* 52-53, 14 April 2010.

Chapter 3

Public finance management system and domestic financial support to the water supply and sanitation sector in Moldova

This chapter presents data on financial flows that represent domestic support to the water supply and sanitation (WSS) sector in Moldova on the supply and demand side, i.e. to WSS systems and operators on the one hand, and to customers on the other hand.

Most domestic financial support to WSS is provided through the public finance management (PFM) system – both on the demand and supply sides. Its key features and the role in funding WSS are discussed in this chapter. Specifically, an in-depth overview of the public finance system and recent trends thereof is provided, including the Medium-Term Budget Framework (MTBF) and the institutional layers. The financial flows in the WSS sector are also inventoried and described as far as the State and district budgets allocations are concerned, as well as other players like the Ministry of Environment (MOE), Ministry of Regional Development and Construction (MRDC) and the special funds. A special section described donors' support activities in the WSS funding schemes. And finally, the social support to end-users of WSS services as part of the PFM system is addressed covering such aspects as the tariff regulation, and the role of central governments, local public administrations (LPAs) and communities in it.

3.1. Overview of the Public Finance system

In a modern economy, the budget is no longer a simple document that indicates only annual expected revenues and expenditures; rather, it is a financial plan at the macroeconomic level. The budgetary process envisions the impact of government operations on the economy and consequent adjustments to the budget. In the new vision of budgeting (i.e. programme-based result-oriented budgeting), it provides much more than economic impact.

The Ministry of Finance (MOF) is the key agency responsible for effective operation of the PFM system in Moldova. Although MOF does not directly manage financial allocations to the WSS sector, it plays an important role nonetheless. First, MOF helps design the MTBF, which presents sector ceilings for three years. Second, MOF facilitates the performance-based (programme-based) budgeting principles; this requires all budget allocations be presented in line with expected outcomes and outputs. Therefore, the government's policy and specific plans for any sector (including WSS) must be transparently presented in the budget. Later, the same information in the budget is monitored and analysed using performance indicators (PIs). Therefore, WSS sector plans and policies must be well incorporated into the budget. This process requires direct facilitation from MOF and adequate capacity in line ministries (MOE and the MRDC in the case of WSS). Finally, if the government expands the inventory of domestic financial and social support mechanisms to the WSS sector, then MOF will provide cross-sector synergies between various instruments aimed at both the supply and demand sides in the WSS sector. MOF is also responsible for financial administration and prepares the government's annual financial reports. The ministry's State Treasury is responsible for money flow and supervises accounting procedures.

The budget cycle and its calendar illustrate the sequence of steps and decisions over various topics that culminate in financial allocations (see Box 3.1).

MOF sets the activities and interim periods of the calendar year. The line ministries co-operate with the central and local public authorities, which in turn are required to co-operate and provide necessary information to specialised authority. Working groups are set to enable this co-operation. Importantly, the MTBF covers not only state budget allocations, but also all sector-related funding, e.g. the section on the WSS sector in the MTBF reflects the state budget funds, extra budgetary funds, local budget funds and, if any, donors' expected expenditures.

Each central public authority uses sector spending limits (ceilings) in the expenditure strategy for planning. However, these ceilings may be revised twice: during the MTBF development stage and during preparations for the annual state budget. Significant deviations in final budget allocations may undermine use of ceilings in the strategic planning stage.

Box 3.1. **Main activities and deadlines for budget development and approval**

Budget schedule (excerpt)

The main activities and deadlines for budget development and approval are the following:

- The government approves and submits the draft law on the medium-term macro-budget limits to Parliament and, if necessary, the draft law amending and completing certain legislative acts *(1 June).*
- Parliament adopts the law on the medium-term macro-budget limits and, if necessary, the amendments and additions to laws deriving from the budget and fiscal policy for the next year *(15 July).*
- The government approves and submits annual budgets to Parliament *(15 October).*
- Parliament adopts annual budget laws *(1 December).*
- Local executive authorities of the second level (see below) prepare and submit draft local budgets to local councils *(15 November)*, and to local executive authorities of the first level *(20 November).*
- The second level local councils adopt respective local budgets *(5 December)* and the first level local councils adopt respective budgets *(10 December).*

Source : Government of Moldova, Budget calendar.

The budget system is an integral part of the public finance system of the state, forms the national public budget and includes the following:

- the state budget
- the local public administrations (LPA) budgets
- The state social insurance budget (SSIB)
- The compulsory medical insurance funds (CMIF).

Figure 3.1 presents the structure of the 2014 national public budget (revenues and expenditures).

Figure 3.1. **Structure of the 2014 National Public Budget (revenue and expenditures)**

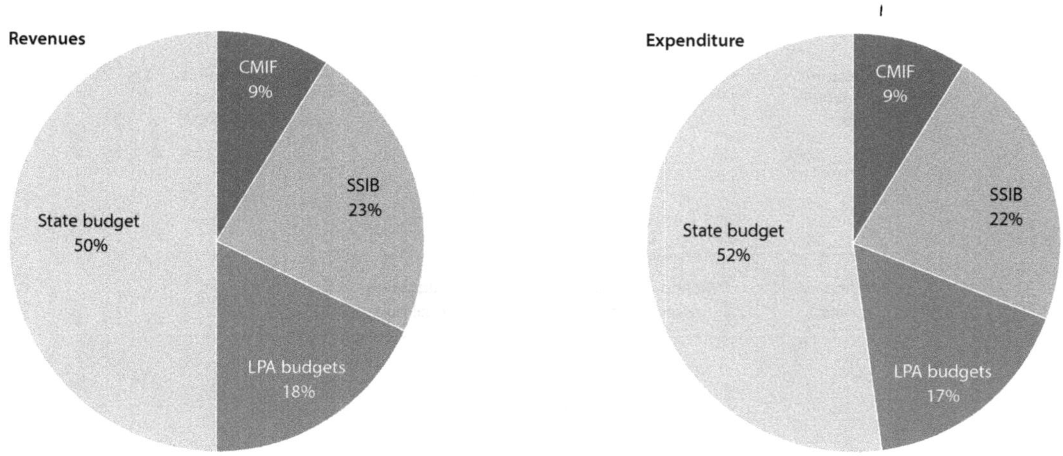

Source: Authors' own elaboration based on Ministry of Finance, Draft annual state budget for 2014.

The state budget expenditures in the WSS sector are mainly capital expenditures. Therefore, MOF and relevant ministries identify priorities for capital investments. Then MOF consults with the relevant working group on objectives, policies and priority projects within the MTBF framework. This is then submitted for approval to the MTBF Steering Group. As indicated above, the decisions over the cross-sector expenditure priorities and sector policies are scaled up to the political level.

As noted in Table 3.1, Moldova has come close to staying on budget over the last three years, with planned and actual spending differing by no more than 1.5%. The fiscal discipline of individual sections is less stable (e.g. the state budget execution level was more than 2% lower than the plan). However, they are all within the internationally accepted range for fluctuation. See "PEFA – PFM Performance Measurement Framework", scoring requirements for PI-1 indicator (www.pefa.org).

Table 3.1. **Public budget plans and actual spending, 2011-13, in MDL**

	2011		2012		2013	
	Plan	Actual	Plan	Actual	Plan	Actual
Central	20 354 074 076	20 004 145 514	22 164 269 100	21 675 321 323	23 611 476 200	23 901 196 485
District (rayons)	7 842 099 230	8 187 209 654	8 855 300 682	8 965 603 131	9 045 985 613	9 608 470 997
Other	12 977 500 000	12 849 200 000	13 865 814 700	13 703 783 100	15 085 100 000	14 961 400 000
Total	**41 173 673 306**	**41 040 555 167**	**44 885 384 482**	**44 344 707 554**	**47 742 561 813**	**48 471 067 482**

Source: Based on BOOST database, http://wbi.worldbank.org/boost/boost-initiative.

MTBF-Budget framework

The medium-term budget planning covers all public revenues and expenditures. The MTBF changed the planning process in Moldova, establishing a strategic and comprehensive method of planning the public money that covers all elements of the national public budget. In addition, the MTBF introduced an initial strategic phase to the budget planning process that takes place before the detailed budget estimates are prepared (see Figure 3.2).

Figure 3.2. **MTBF-Budget process**

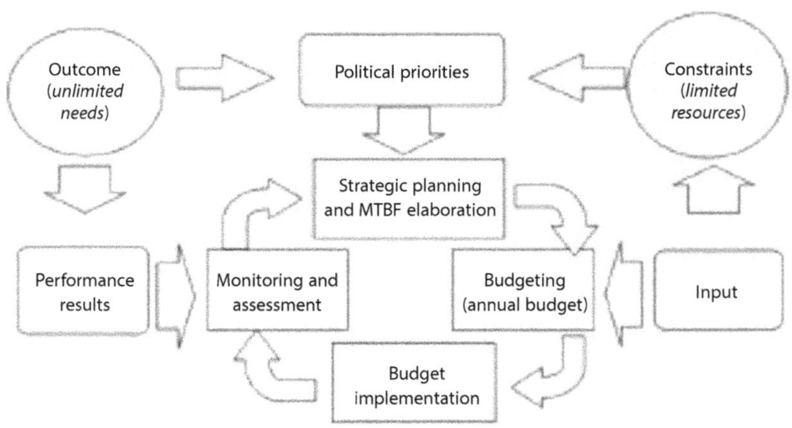

Source: Based on authors' findings.

The MTBF ensures the allocation of funds aligns with policy priorities. It provides downward estimates of resources available to cover public expenditures, along with upward estimates of costs for actual (or planned) policies. The annual budget law is developed based on these priorities and considers available limited resources. Budget implementation, monitoring and assessment are based on performance results. Annually, under the Law on Public Finance and Budget and Fiscal Responsibility and in accordance with the budget schedule, the government approves the MTBF. It includes the budget and fiscal policy objectives, as well as a medium-term forecast of funds and expenditures of the national public budget and its components.

The MTBF forecasts are updated annually and extended by one year, maintaining the three-year perspective in budget planning. The policy priorities and the spending limits in the MTBF form the basis for public authorities to develop budget proposals/draft budgets for the next fiscal year. To ensure transparency and participation in developing the MTBF, and to facilitate co-operation between public authorities, a series of working groups involves multiple concerned parties. The formation and approval of these groups, membership and tasks are described in the legal framework.

The central public administrations (ministries, agencies, etc.) develop and approve their own schedule of activities in line with recommendations on the internal organisation of the MTBF development and their annual budgets. This enables them to implement actions and comply with deadlines for the MTBF development and approval, as well as to internally organise activities related to development of sector-expenditure strategies.

The WSS sector has been included in the MTBF process since the 2009 budget year as part of the environment protection sector strategy.

Apacanal services are not financed directly from the budget. Therefore, they are not part of the current budget process. However, they are mostly publicly owned organisations and, in a wider context, are part of the public financial management system of the country. Thus, their activities and financial performance must become part of the national reporting system on public finance, if and when modern accounting standards and requirements on financial statements are introduced.

3.2. Key domestic actors providing support to the WSS sector

Both national and local actors in the public sector provide support to the WSS sector, directly from the public budget and from dedicated funds.

The two main funds operating in the WSS sector are environmental funds (local and national) and the National Fund for Regional Development (NFRD).

Environmental Funds

Environmental Funds, used for collecting and spending money to solve environmental problems, are organised on two levels:

- The National Environmental Fund (NEF), also known as the Eco Funds, is administrated by the accounting and audit unit within the fund administration at the central level.
- Local Environmental Funds are administrated by the fund's secretariat at the local level.

The decisions on awarding grants and contracts from the funds belong to administrative councils, which are created at both the national and local level. Each environmental fund can make autonomous decisions, but 30% of revenues from the Local Environmental Funds are transferred to the NEF.

The Ministry of Environment (MOE) co-ordinates the activities of Local Environmental Funds. The co-operation is primarily administered by the territorial Environmental inspections; effective co-operation among the institutions is still a challenge. The ministry is enhancing its capacities for effective management of projects by establishing an Investment Unit.

Between 2004-13, spending from environmental funds has increased substantially: from MDL 4.8 million to MDL 406.7 million. This increase is due to improving the tax base, especially from introducing new fees for packaging materials in 2008. Consequently, the share of revenues from fees for emissions has decreased.

A significant challenge is the absorption of available resources. The lack of absorptive capacity results in outstanding cash in the fund accounts at the end of the fiscal period. The new budget policy envisages the possibility of retaining the unspent resources, which creates a major risk to the volume of financial flows in the sector.

Table 3.2. **NEF financial trends, in millions of MDL**

	2012 actual	2013 actual	2014 planned
Revenues	235.6	248.1	208.3
Expenditures	202.6	406.7	248.3

Source: Government of Moldova, *National Environmental Fund Reports*, 2012-14.

Spending in 2013 increased significantly because fund administrators used money left over from the previous year. The WSS system received a substantial allocation from the environmental funds. The nominal amount is increasing, along with the number of projects financed (Table 3.3). Setting clear performance targets, monitoring results and assessing performance, however, remain a challenge.

Table 3.3. **NEF expenditures in the WSS sector**

	2010	2011	2012	2013
Number of projects	70	100	83	177
Allocation for WSS, in MDL millions	89.6	112.7	132.8	298.7

Source: Ministry of Environment Annual Report, 2013.

The Minister of Environment regulates decision making on selection of projects and financial allocations (Figure 3.3). These phases are not implemented properly because the legal framework is neither clear nor consistent, while supervision capacities are very low as well. For Local Environmental Funds, the most important deficiency is the advertising phase. For the NEF, lack of clear performance targets makes it difficult to assess cost effectiveness of expenditures for WSS.

Figure 3.3. **Project cycle within the National Environmental Fund**

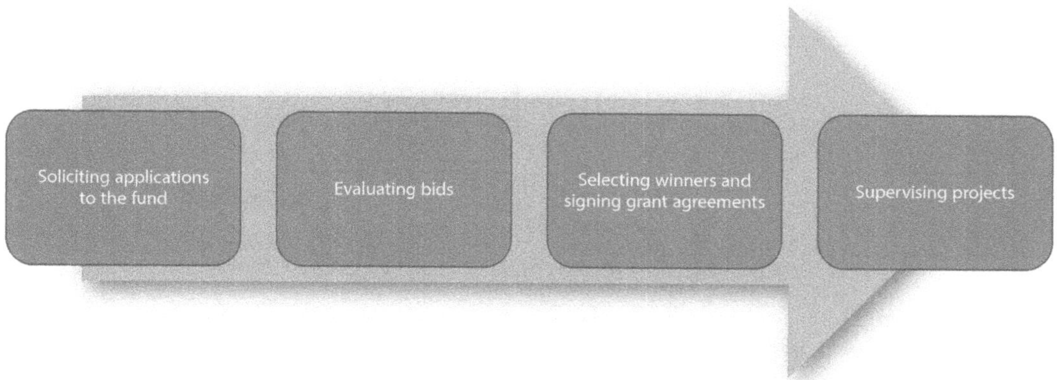

Source: Based on authors' findings.

The National Fund for Regional Development

The National Fund for Regional Development (NFRD) has a designated allocation of 1% of revenues in the annual budget under the Ministry of Regional Development and Construction. This fund is a main source of financing for regional development agencies.

Table 3.4 presents the planning process of the budget and awarding of contracts.

Table 3.4. **Timetable of the budgeting process by the NFRD**

	Sept.	Oct.	Nov.	Dec.	Jan.	Feb.	March	April	May	June	July	Aug.
Budget calendar	Annual budget law approval						Budget limits approval			Finalising the draft budget		
Advertising campaign	■											
Receiving bid proposals		■										
Evaluation of bids		■										
Approval of proposals by the Regional Council			■									
Evaluation of proposals by the Evaluation Committee				■	■							
Final approval of proposals by the National Council for Regional Development						■	■					
Formal approval for contract implementation							■	■				

Source: Operational Manual on using funds from NFRD approved by Decision No. 4/12 dated 23 February 2012.

The fund is operated through the state treasury, which receives the budget allocation on the fund's behalf. It also generates other revenues such as interest from investments, donations and grants. Figure 3.4 illustrates the operating environment for the fund.

Regional Development Agencies administer financial operations for investment projects via territorial treasury branches. The Regional Council for Development is an advisory body, but not a legal entity. It consists of a head of rayon councils, mayors, representatives from private sector and civil society.

Figure 3.4. **Institutional and operational environment for the National Fund for Regional Development**

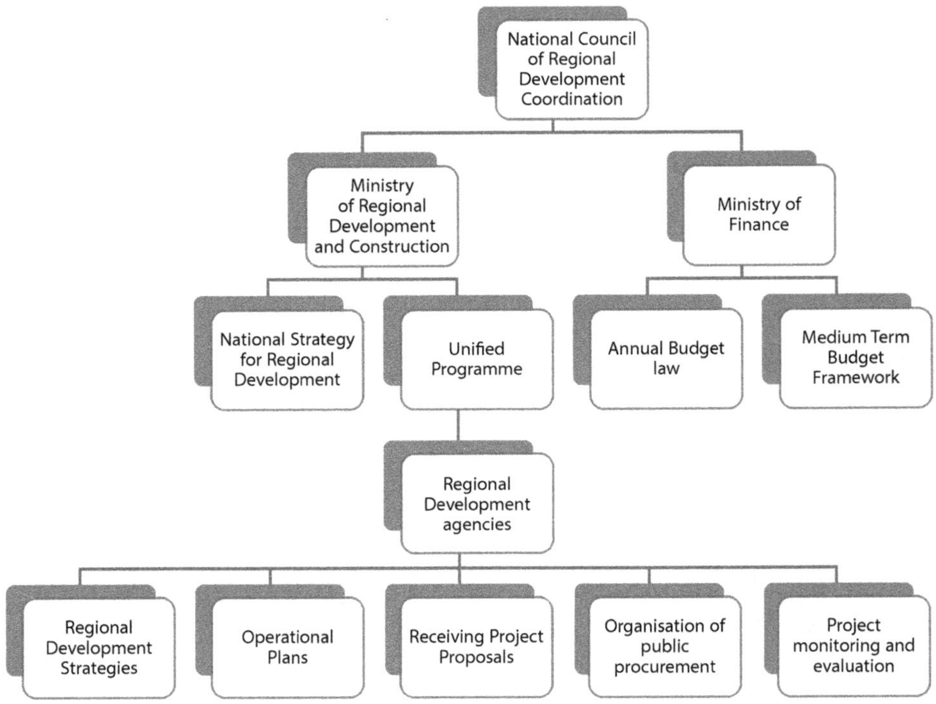

Source: Based on authors' findings.

All approved projects are included in the Unified Programme. The NFRD develops regional water supply and sewage infrastructure as one of the main dimensions of its operation. It has clear and measurable targets and performance indicators. This makes it possible and relatively easy to measure cost effectiveness of its spending for WSS (e.g. how many km of distribution pipes were built, or new consumers connected to the system per MDL I million spent, etc.).

Municipalities

There are two levels of local public administration (LPA):

- level I (lowest) – around 900 villages and communes
- level II – 32 rayons (districts), ATU Gagauz Yeri and two municipalities (Chisinau and Balti).

The responsibilities for WSS remain with LPA level I and with municipalities of Chisinau and Balti. Gagauz Yeri has a separate public administration structure.

After recent amendments to the legislation on social support system, local authorities are the only authorities. They may allocate compensation or other form of direct social support in the WSS sector to households. Such transfers may be funded from the LPA's own budget resources.

3.3. Inventory of domestic financial support to the WSS sector

There are various sources of domestic funding in the WSS sector in Moldova, including state and municipal budgets (including through in-budget funds), households, businesses and donors. There are also some domestic financial support mechanisms, but of a limited nature.

Allocations for the WSS sector from state, rayon and municipal budgets:

The main agencies managing state budget financial flows in the WSS sector are the Ministry of Environment and its subordinated agencies; the Ministry of Regional Development and Construction and its subordinated agencies; and the Ministry of Finance. Some parts of these funds come from the special (dedicated) funds in the state budget:

- The National Environmental Fund (NEF)
- The National Fund for Regional Development (NFRD).

The budget system may not be able to trace some investments in the WSS sector due to their secondary nature. For example, expenditures will not be classified as "WSS sector" when a water supply system is built in a public school or a hospital. Several budget categories, however, do allow to trace WSS expenditures:

- 11.04 Water service
- 12.01 Environment protection
- 15.02 Utilities.

The category 11.04 "Water service" includes expenditures in irrigation; indeed, in 2013, Apele Moldovei spent the entire budget for this category on irrigation. Most of the WSS sector financial data below 11.04 is not identified. In addition, significant misclassifications also exist in the "15.02 Utilities" category of the LPA budgets. This may have some impact on the accuracy of the data presented in this report. At the same time, these are official data published in the BOOST database, which is endorsed by MOF. The overall trends for WSS state budget expenditures are presented in Table 3.5.

Table 3.5. **Actual state budget allocations for WSS under different budget categories (lines)**

	2009	2010	2011	2012	2013
12.01 Environment protection	132 155 902	155 407 684	190 515 009	238 466 878	326 717 257
15.02 Utilities	2 147 250	38 888 779	123 508 006	139 048 224	329 504 858
Total WSS	**134 303 152**	**194 296 463**	**314 023 016**	**377 515 102**	**656 222 115**

Source: Based on BOOST database, http://wbi.worldbank.org/boost/boost-initiative.

The allocations for the sector have different financing sources, e.g. the state's own resources and donor funds. The WSS projects are administrated via "Apele Moldovei", the NFRD and the National Environmental Fund, or, sometimes, channelled directly by donors out of the treasury system. Donors may operate outside of the treasury system; accessing comprehensive information on those donor funds might be challenging.

The WSS sector is heavily funded through public budgets (central and district/rayon). Overall, the sector receives around 2% of public funds (consolidated state and district budgets). Calculations are based on functional classification of the central and district budgets (subcategories 12.01 – Environment protection and 15.02 – Utilities). Figure 3.5 indicates that commitments to the sector exceeded actual allocations prior to 2012; since then, the sector has started to receive significantly more than planned.

Figure 3.5. **Budget and actual allocations for the Moldovan water and sanitation sector, 2009-13**

as a % of the total

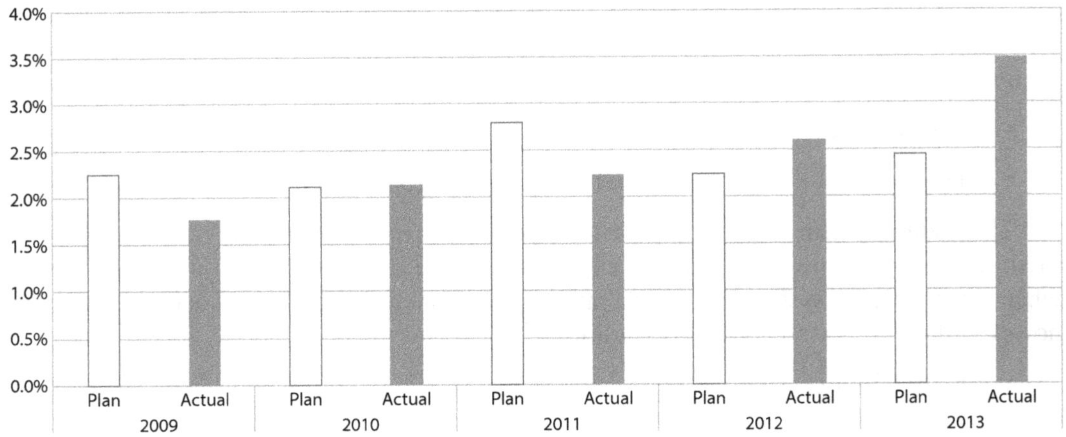

Source: Based on BOOST database, http://wbi.worldbank.org/boost/boost-initiative.

A closer look into the breakdown of these data indicates that the state budget, as a rule, is allocating less than planned (except in 2013); the rayon budgets showed increasing allocations for WSS in the period reviewed (except 2011) – see Figure 3.6. While the role of WSS in the central budget has remained stable over the years (with some fluctuations between the planned and actual figures), the role of WSS expenditures in district (rayon) budgets has gradually increased from 6% to more than 10% between 2009-13.

Figure 3.6. **Allocations for WSS from the central and rayon budgets in 2009-13, MDL**

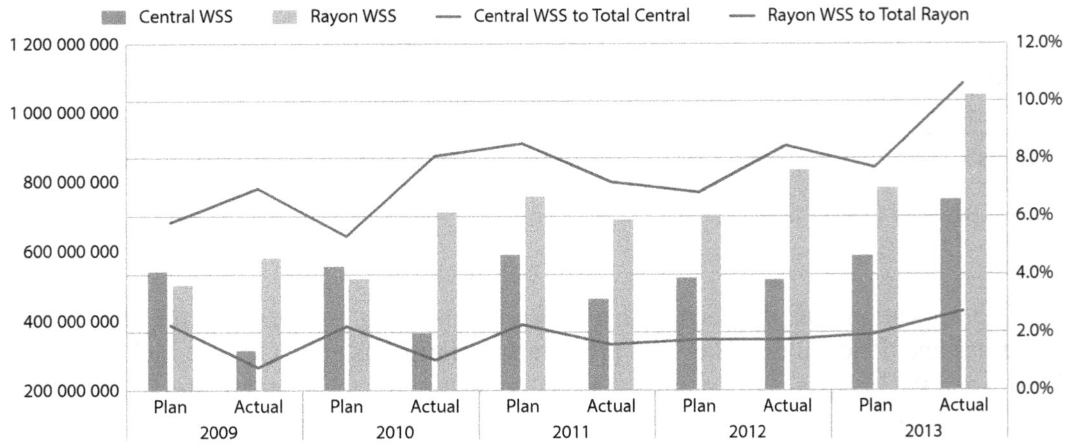

Source: Based on BOOST database, http://wbi.worldbank.org/boost/boost-initiative.

In Figure 3.7, the same data for districts by development regions indicate that an identical pattern of allocating more than planned in all three "development regions".

Figure 3.7. **Allocations for WSS sector by rayons in development regions in 2010-13, MDL**

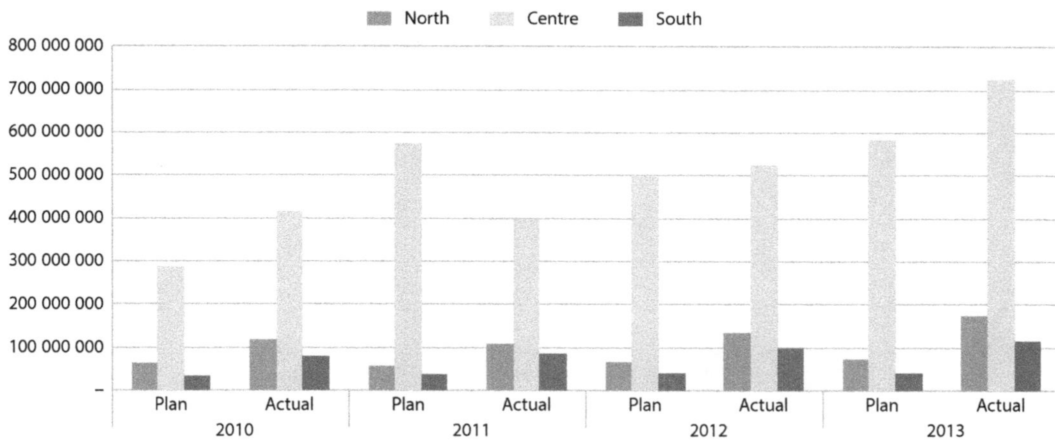

Source: Based on BOOST database, http://wbi.worldbank.org/boost/boost-initiative.

Data for the central development region in Figure 3.7 include the Chisinau municipality. If excluded, the pattern will be more balanced (see Figure 3.8). However, the several fold difference between planned and actual expenditure still remains.

Figure 3.8. **Allocations to WSS sector by municipalities (excluding Chisinau) in development regions, 2010-13**

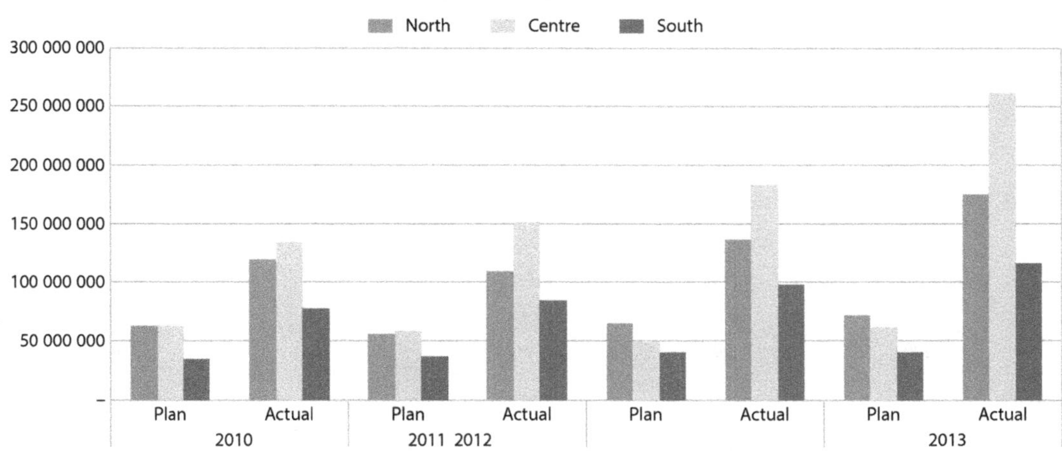

Source: Based on BOOST database, http://wbi.worldbank.org/boost/boost-initiative.

All above data indicate too much flexibility throughout the fiscal year on allocations to the WSS sector by districts/municipalities. Some changes in planning might be required to make the process more smooth and predictable. As indicated in the sections above, there is no significant issue with overall fiscal discipline in Moldova, either at central or district budget levels. Therefore, significant discrepancies between planned and actual allocations for WSS (towards over-execution) indicate poor planning rather than lack of absorption capacity.

Figure 3.9 indicates the share of capital expenditures in state budget allocations for the WSS sector has more than doubled between 2009 and 2013, increasing from 30% to more than 70%.

Figure 3.9. **Breakdown of state budget expenditures for WSS by type, 2009-13**

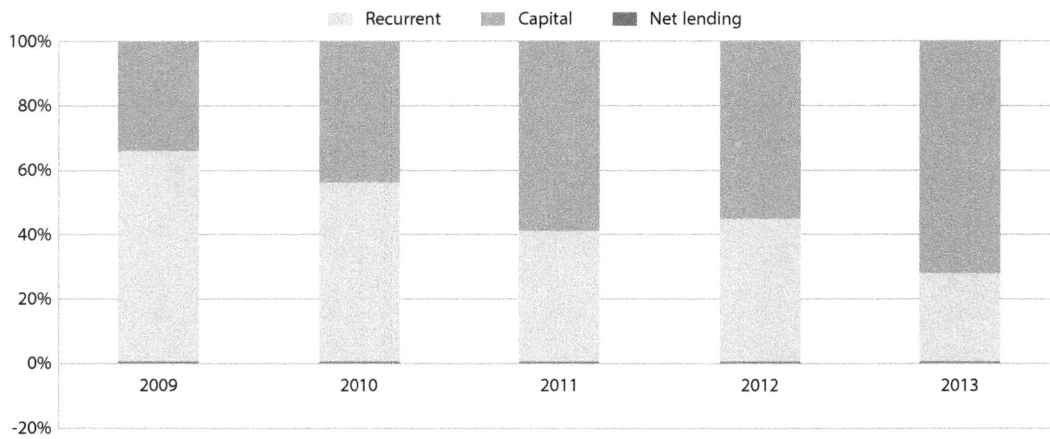

Source: Based on BOOST database, http://wbi.worldbank.org/boost/boost-initiative.

In Figure 3.10, the same breakdown for district budgets shows the latter has remained more stable; over 50% of allocations for WSS are still of a recurrent nature.

Figure 3.10. **Breakdown of district budget WSS expenditures by type, 2009-13**

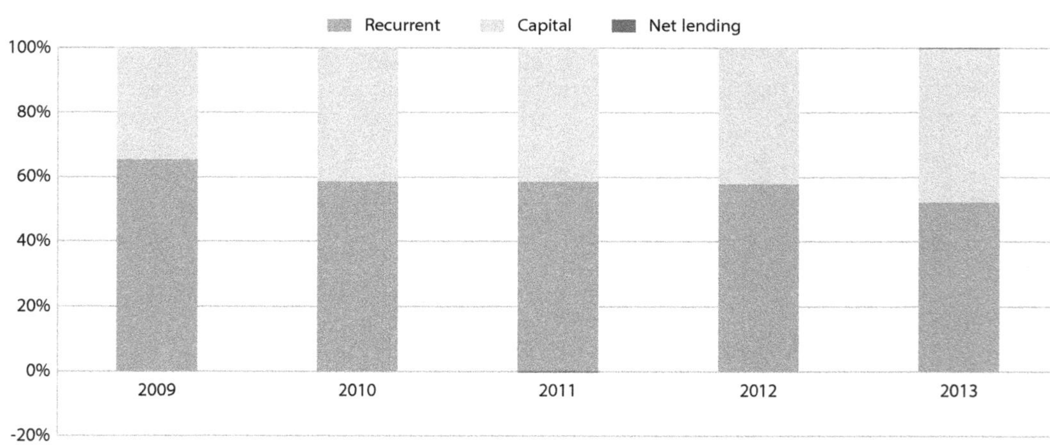

Source: Based on BOOST database, http://wbi.worldbank.org/boost/boost-initiative.

The two main special (dedicated) funds (NEF and NFRD) are part of the state budget. However, the role of these funds in actual state budget expenditures in WSS-related programmes is significant in both of the main agencies involved in the sector. Therefore, information on those funds is presented separately.

Ministry of Environment

Overall budget allocations for WSS by the Ministry of Environment (MOE) have significantly increased in the last four years (see Figure 3.11).

Figure 3.11. **Actual budget allocations by the Ministry of Environment for the WSS sector, 2010-13**

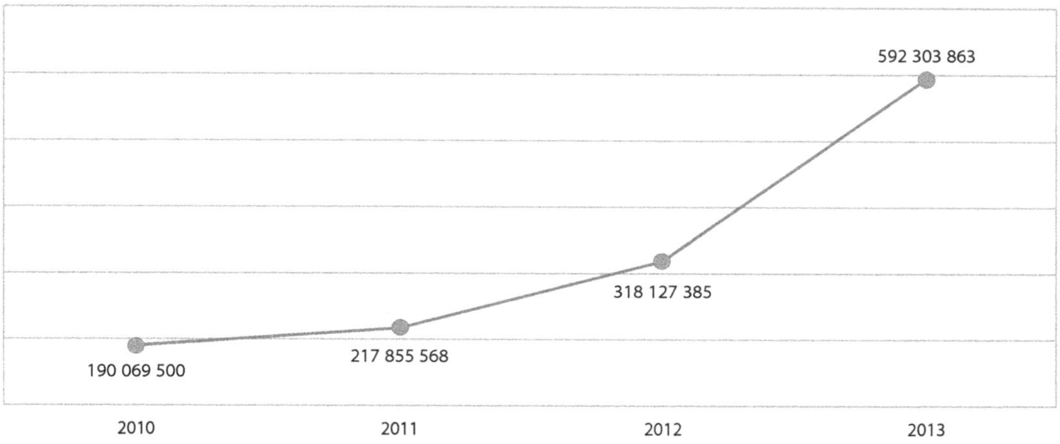

Source: Based on BOOST database, http://wbi.worldbank.org/boost/boost-initiative.

The National Environmental Fund also plays a significant role in allocations for WSS by the Ministry of Environment. Unlike for the Ministry of Regional Development and Construction, the state budget funds more than ten various programmes in the WSS sector led by the MOE. Of all these programmes, the NEF plays the most significant role, spending around half of all MOE allocations for WSS (see Figure 3.12). The Water Supply Service Development Program (funded by the European Bank for Reconstruction and Development [EBRD],

Figure 3.12. **Actual WSS budget allocations via the Ministry of Environment, by programme, 2010-13**

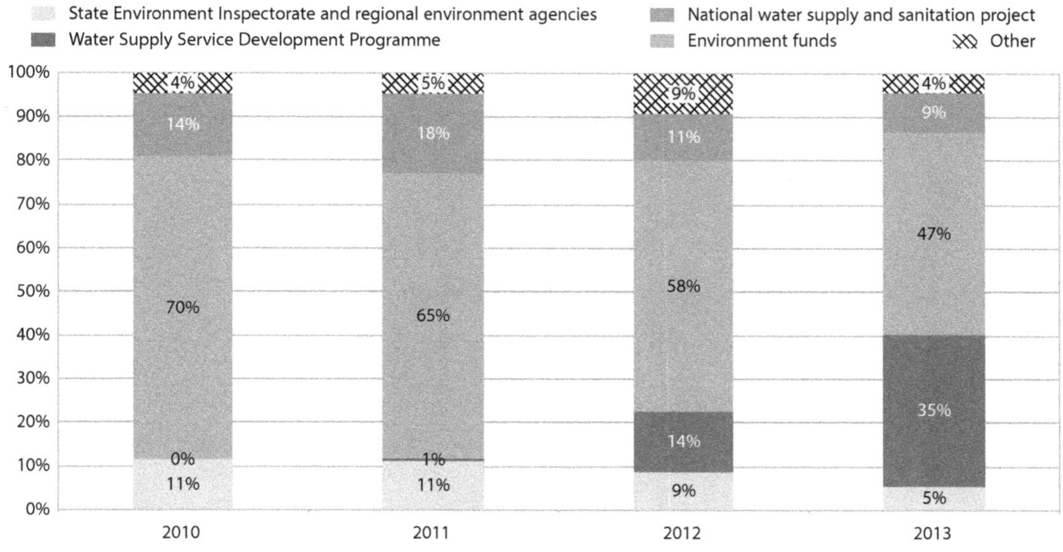

Source: Based on BOOST database, http://wbi.worldbank.org/boost/boost-initiative.

European Investment Bank [EIB], European Neighbourhood and Partnership Instrument grant and the EU Neighbourhood Investment Facility) has recently become the second biggest programme: it has had a significant impact not only on the composition of budget allocations, but also the total amounts. The third biggest programme was the WB-funded National Water Supply and Sanitation Project, which was completed in 2013.

As indicated in Figure 3.11, MOE has more than tripled actual allocations to the WSS sector over the four years between 2010 and 2013. The two main driving factors were the doubling of NEF allocations and introducing the Water Supply Service Development Program in 2012.

The amounts in Figure 3.12 also reflect allocations for Apele Moldovei, a water agency within MOE. The agency's role in the WSS sector is important, as indicated by Table 3.6, which summarises the sector's financial flows.

Table 3.6 indicates that 70% of total actual allocations of Apele Moldovei in 2013 were in the irrigation sector; the rest were allocated to the environmental funds. The three main categories of expenditures relate to capital investments in various forms – 21% for capital investments themselves, 55% for purchasing fixed assets and 23% for capital transfers within Moldova.

Table 3.6. **Apele Moldovei financial flows in 2010-13**

in MDL thousands

	2010	2011	2012	2013
Operation of irrigation systems	**15 972 500**	**19 702 500**	**17 100 500**	**12 972 500**
Environment funds			**1 115 156**	**5 204 962**
Remuneration of staff			8 700	
Mandatory state social insurance premiums			2 001	
Payment for goods and services			1 104 151	
Employer's share of the mandatory health insurance premiums			305	
Capital investments				1 101 000
Purchase of fixed assets				2 886 000
Capital transfers within country				1 217 962
Better water supply for six pilot districts of the Republic of Moldova project	**819 227**			
Total	**16 791 727**	**19 702 500**	**18 215 656**	**18 177 462**

Source: Based on BOOST database, http://wbi.worldbank.org/boost/boost-initiative.

Ministry of Regional Development and Construction

Table 3.7 shows that nearly 100% of all actual WSS expenditures by the Ministry of Regional Development and Construction are made through the NFRD.

Table 3.7. **Breakdown of MRDC actual expenditures by programmes, 2010-13**

	2010	2011	2012	2013
Ministry of Regional Development and Construction (total)	203 123 045	264 955 055	337 331 868	343 194 294
Ministry of Regional Development and Construction (WSS)	1 777 363	96 167 448	59 387 717	63 918 252
Urban planning/development in municipalities			993 480	
Emergencies and coping with consequences of natural disasters		6 807 596	765 744	3 923 580
National Fund for Regional Development	1 777 363	89 359 853	57 628 493	59 265 308
Local public services modernisation project				729 364
Ministry of Regional Development and Construction (WSS to total in percentage)	1%	36%	18%	19%

Source: Based on BOOST database, http://wbi.worldbank.org/boost/boost-initiative.

3.4. Social support to end-users of WSS services as part of the PFM system

Requirements on social support system for WSS

In WSS, addressing a number of specific social issues will be a challenge considering the limited capacity of the overall social support system in Moldova.

Right to water

Access to sufficient, safe and affordable water without discrimination has been internationally recognised as a universal human right. The main resolutions in this respect were passed by the UN General Assembly and the UN Human Rights Council resolutions, both in 2010. Adoption of the 2030 Agenda for Sustainable Development in September 2015 has re-affirmed the policy objective. Consequently, governments bear a more direct responsibility for the provision of drinking water to socially vulnerable groups. It is not sufficient to delegate this responsibility purely to social ministries.

Indeed, general social policies may make water affordable, but cannot make it accessible, safe and sufficient. This illustrates the need for WSS policy to strengthen DFSMs aimed at both supporting the demand for, and supply of, WSS services (especially demand from vulnerable social groups) and improving the supply of quality WSS services in Moldova.

Need for targeted financial and social assistance in WSS

Lack of access to WSS services is a significant factor in sustaining high levels of poverty because of its effect on human health and household income. Water and poverty are so closely related that there is a need (and an opportunity) to address it from within the sector.

Presently, the benefits of water and sanitation are spread unevenly: typically urban centres have better access and higher quality WSS than rural areas. Extra expenses for bottled water are a consequence of the lack of access to drinking water of sufficient quality. Costs of bottled water for rural households are much higher than those for piped drinking water, aggravating the poverty-sustaining effect of lack of access.

Therefore, social policies must be incorporated into the overall WSS policy and financial support mechanisms (especially domestic ones) must also be part of this overall policy framework.

However, a social ministry alone cannot provide targeted (social) assistance; WSS systems extension is not its responsibility, while ensuring the supply of drinking water is a major social policy measure in itself. Support of the demand side, i.e. supporting consumers via subsidies, financial allowances, discounts or other social support mechanisms may not always transform into a well-defined demand for increased network coverage. Consumers may not show rational behaviour in self-organising for long-lasting policies or responding positively to water sector operators' long-term investment policies. This is where the government's support in increasing the network via state budget allocations and consolidated donor support can play a critical role.

Therefore, the government needs to continue its financial support to WSS organisations in rehabilitating and expanding the network and investing in infrastructure development (supply-side financial support mechanism). Communities and municipalities, especially in rural areas, may not have enough financial resources and long-term investment capacities to organise the above processes.

However, given that subsidies in WSS sectors occur in various forms, public interventions may not necessarily benefit the poor. Unwise distribution of public resources may benefit rich households (or businesses) that have access to and consume water more than socially vulnerable households that do not have access or consume with more care. Therefore, demand-side financial and social support mechanisms need to be well-tailored and targeted at the households that really need such support.

Overall, supply-side measures will enable the government to address current WSS challenges in Moldova. These include limited access to piped water supplies in rural areas, or the need for improving the quality of piped water. Meanwhile, demand-side measures must address the affordability challenges. **A combination of both the demand- and supply-side support mechanisms will enable comprehensive coverage and effective application of domestic financial support mechanisms.**

Tariff measures

Many countries employ indirect social support mechanisms such as **cross subsidy**, which can be achieved via block tariffs, differentiated tariffs to households vs. businesses, etc. Service providers use the latter mechanism with some active regulatory and policymaking role of the central or local governments. The central and municipal governments also use direct social support mechanisms, which are usually reflected in the budgets.

However, the methodology of the National Agency for Regulation in Energy (ANRE) does not integrate social factors. Nor does it establish links with appropriate social support measures that should be provided more effectively and efficiently through mechanisms other than tariffs. Of course, as the regulator, ANRE itself should not provide such support. Other actors of a sound regulatory system, such as the Ministry of Social Affairs and/or LPAs, are well placed to play this role. Observations below suggest this key element is largely missing in Moldova, however.

Central government

The central government pays no social allowances related to the WSS sector. The reforms in 2009 foresaw substitution of the social allowances by introducing a new social support payment to eligible households. These reforms were planned to be implemented in stages. Only households with disabled people were eligible for the programme during the first stage. Then families with children and pensioners were allowed to apply for social support. In mid-2010, all households received the right to apply for the new social support.

At the same time, entrance of new beneficiaries into the existing social allowance system was prohibited. Previously eligible beneficiaries received support until the end of 2012. Meanwhile, new procedures for supporting peoples with special needs were developed.

LPAs and communities

The nominal social allowances by central government were fully cancelled as of the 2012 fiscal year. However, municipal/local authorities now have the right to provide social compensations within available local budgets. But this study could not identify any significant indication of systemic social support mechanisms at the municipal level.

Interviewed stakeholders occasionally mentioned *ad hoc* assistance to vulnerable groups. For instance, Chisinau municipality partially subsidises heating costs for low-income households. In rural settlements, there are also cases where beneficiaries self-organise and set some mutual support mechanisms, especially during installations of local WSS systems.

However, a small number of survey responses from municipalities indicated no social support mechanisms channelled through local budgets. The survey was not representative for the country, however. In any case, it appears that relevant local financial/social support mechanisms in the WSS sector are insignificant in Moldova, even for those municipalities that have such ad hoc cases.

Apacanals (as business entities in public property)

Feedback from the 12 Apacanals reaffirms initial responses from stakeholders about the insignificance of direct social income support from operators in the WSS sector. According to the survey of 12 Apacanals, only two companies provide grants to customers with total of MDL 1.5 million (0.2% compared with total sales).Examples of various cross-subsidy mechanisms (e.g. from businesses to households) in the sector, are discussed in more detail in the following chapter on social support systems in Moldova related to WSS.

3.5. Concluding remarks

Existing strategies put heavy accent on investment needs (both from donors and the state budget). However, financial statements of Apacanals indicate the sector generates significant losses every year; this is a policy change for the sector. Someone pays (or will pay) for those losses, even if it is not explicit in the state and rayon budgets. Ultimately, the whole population pays. Attracting lots of new investments (including grants) does not solve the core problem as the sector cannot afford the current policy. As in many other countries (e.g. Armenia), explicit or implicit subsidy of the supply side for Moldova shifts the state financial support from poor households to richer ones; this is another factor to consider while adjusting the current public financing policy in the WSS sector in Moldova.

Subsidies for the WSS sector must be done wisely and with the larger context of the country in mind. In some cases, operators may need support from the state to expand the network (as the population will hardly self-organise itself for long-term projects). In other cases, the sector may need support due to significant demographic shifts that break up the whole pattern of estimated vs. actual demand for water. Technology is another dimension to consider, as old water consumption norms and design norms for WSS systems may no longer be relevant. Price elasticity of the demand for water may also play a significant role that affects optimal tariff levels.

Therefore, public financial support to the WSS sector is sometimes unavoidable. However, choice of the intervention mechanism is important. Otherwise, the millions of leis invested in the WSS sector may be largely wasted.

Another conclusion is that WSS sector decision making in Moldova (especially in investing activities) is quite fragmented – from MOE and its NEF on the one hand to MRDC and the RDF on the other. The two funds seem to operate independently, but with significant room for better co-ordination. In addition, the donor community is also a significant player in the sector with only a fraction of funds channelled through the national PFM systems, as presented above.

Finally, the overall political economy of the sector is further complicated by the absence of coherent planning systems and processes that would incorporate the sectoral and the national and sub-national (regional) planning systems. The latter is quite important, as top-down decisions may not always reflect the real needs of local administrations. Therefore, a synergy between the top-down and bottom-up planning systems must be generated, foremost in the development regions.

References

BOOST database, http://wbi.worldbank.org/boost/boost-initiative.

Government of Moldova, Budget calendar.

Government of Moldova, *National Environmental Fund Reports*, 2012-14.

Government of Moldova (2013), *Ministry of Environment Annual Report.*

Government of Moldova, *Operational Manual on using funds from NFRD*, approved by Decision No. 4/12 dated 23 February 2012.

Note on references: in the Republic of Moldova, all official documents that are public (Ordinances, Decisions, Strategies etc.) approved by the Parliament, President or Government are published in the *Official Monitor* journal in Moldovan/Romanian and in Russian, http://monitorul.md.

Chapter 4

Social support systems in Moldova related to water supply and sanitation

This chapter presents social support systems in Moldova related to water supply and sanitation (WSS) (direct and indirect support, on the supply and demand side) and assesses them.

The main conclusions are that the water-related social support system is under-developed, lacks specific focus on the poor and effectiveness, and the support measures that are used most heavily in Moldova (e.g. cross-subsidies) provide little value for money. Three social support systems that perform relatively well are all much smaller in size. It is therefore recommended to strengthen the system using good international experience, including from reference countries (see Chapter 5).

Previous chapters considered the need to use various effective mechanisms to channel public financial support to address social issues within the WSS sector. The chapters conclude that WSS actors must carry out part of WSS-related social support measures. Action may be required, but what is already happening in Moldova? How do these measures compare to the reference countries? This is the subject of Chapters 4 and 5.

Before describing actual WSS-related social measures in Moldova, the chapter provides a brief institutional overview of the social support sector.

4.1. Institutional framework and legal background for social measures

A number of laws and decisions are relevant with respect to social aspects of WSS in Moldova. Box 4.1 below presents the most important ones.

Box 4.1. **Legal background for social measures**

From 2000, Moldova has had a system of targeted compensations for certain vulnerable segments of the population (RM Government Decision No. 761 from 31 July 2000). Small amounts are provided to categories of vulnerable citizens through a mechanism involving the Ministry of Finance, the National Cash Desk Social Insurance and the *Banca de Economii.*

According to the law on local public administration No. 436 – XVI from 28 December 2006 art. 14g, local governments approve tariffs for services. Currently, all tariff schedules contain cross subsidy from industry to households.

From 14 September 2014, Law No. 303 on public water supply and sewer services took effect. The National Agency for Energy Regulation (ANRE) now licenses municipal operators, and develops and approves the methodology for determining, approving and applying tariffs. The agency has indicated that its methodology will not affect social support mechanisms directly or explicitly.

The government has a policy regarding preferential tariffs for penitentiaries (Resolution of the RM Government No. 302 from 12 March 2002 art. 3), as well as for residential care for children from socially disadvantaged families (RM Government Decision No. 865 from 1 August 2007).

In accordance with the law on water (Act No. 272 from 23 December 2011 art. 4 [3]), water belongs to the state, but local public administration shall create, organise and manage the public water supply and sanitation (Law No. 303 from 13 December 2013).

Source : Based on authors' findings.

From the above description one can see that no single body is responsible for social issues in the WSS sector. At the same time, each body is responsible for something that has social dimensions.

A few examples:

The Ministry of Environment is partly responsible for the rehabilitation, upgrade and expansion of networks. The socio-economic benefits of these activities are vast in terms of the beneficiaries' income generation, health, costs savings, use of energy and availability of time. In principle, one would want to evaluate this social return on these investments in WSS against alternative use of financial resources by the government for social purposes. Such a comparison cannot take place at this moment, however.

ANRE, which has become responsible for economic regulation of the water sector as of mid-September 2014, regulates tariffs for rich and poor people alike. Social tariffs for poorer households may be part of a social policy mix. Social benefits may be an efficient use of the available social budget. ANRE, however, does not consider these social aspects of economic regulation. Hence, there is no mechanism to evaluate jointly and subsequently co-ordinate policies to maximise the impact of the social budget.

The Ministry of Regional Development also carries out water investment projects, namely through the Regional Development Agencies and the National Fund for Regional Development (NRDF). In this way, it contributes to the welfare of vulnerable groups through increased access to WSS. However, these measures are not identified as social support measures and therefore cannot be evaluated against alternative uses of the social budget in a broad sense.

The Ministry of Labour, Family and Social Protection is developing a social safety net for the very poorest parts of the population to help pay for WSS expenses. These social expenses cannot be evaluated against alternative social measures, e.g. subsidised use of a limited amount of water or the benefit of increased access. World Bank (2014) has more reflections on the social security system in Moldova.

It is admittedly difficult to compare the social return on various budget lines that are each controlled by different ministries and agencies. Ideally, however, such a comparison would be useful. At the very least, policy makers could compare various policies with social dimensions for the WSS. This is precisely the aim of this chapter.

Social consideration plays an important role in decision making and funds allocation, albeit mostly in an implicit way. So far, only ANRE has excluded social considerations from the tariff methodology. In other countries, such as Kosovo, the economic regulator does consider social aspects of tariffs; social aspects are also considered in Albania. This project aims to jumpstart a similar kind of dialogue in Moldova between the economic regulator and stakeholders.

Given the generally implicit nature of WSS-related social considerations, targets and budgets, it is hard to measure and compare the efficiency and effectiveness of social measures. Still, these measures and flows do exist. The first step is to identify and estimate their impact.

4.2. Affordability

"The human right to water entitles everyone to sufficient, safe, acceptable, physically accessible and affordable water for personal and domestic uses", UN CESC – General Comment 15, para. 2.

From the above adjectives, "affordable" is the one most difficult to measure.

Many donors and development banks active in infrastructure financing consider tariffs for WSS as generally affordable for the population at large as long as the average household bill for these services does not exceed 4% of household expenditure. This study will use this same threshold, which is commonly applied in feasibility studies in European countries. In the context of the relatively low income of Moldova and a high value of water for the population, a threshold of 5% may have to be accepted. Lower income countries necessarily spend more of their income on WSS.

Even with a straightforward affordability definition, two complexities arise. First, no single national affordable tariff can be expressed in MDL/m³. Affordability of tariffs is different because of uneven distribution of income among urban and rural population, and among regions. Furthermore, differences in consumption patterns, influenced by WSS tariffs due to price elasticity of demand (see Figure 4.1), also creates differences in affordability.

Figure 4.1. **Impact of tariff on water consumption in Moldova**

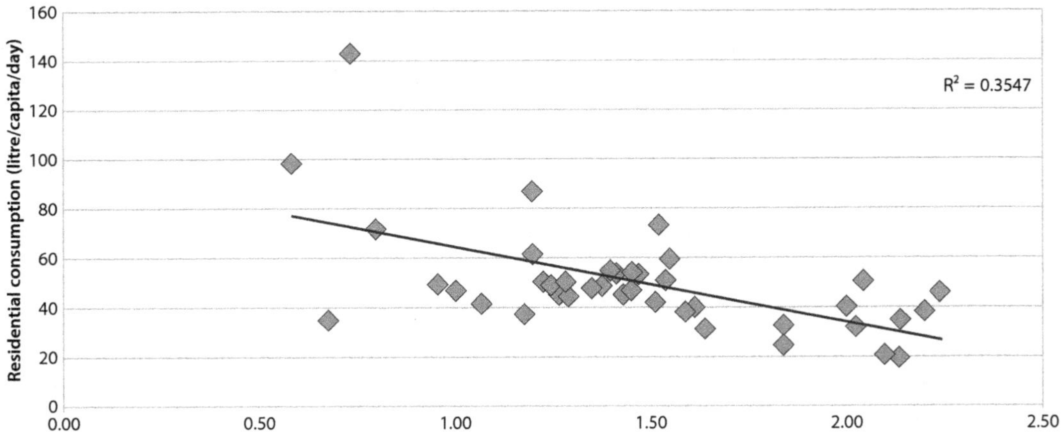

Source: World Bank (2013), based on AMAC data.

Tariffs affordable for the population at large may still be too high for vulnerable groups such as disabled people, pensioners and families with many children. Furthermore, lower overall tariffs will not solve the affordability constraint for everyone. Indeed, they may be a very costly and ineffective approach.

Unfortunately, there is no consensus or best practice defining "vulnerable groups" and the amount of income they may spend on WSS. It is also country-specific and difficult to measure. In Moldova, the situation is extreme; until recently, some 20% of the population was below the official poverty line (Figure 4.2).

Figure 4.2. **Share of the population of Moldova below the official poverty line, %**

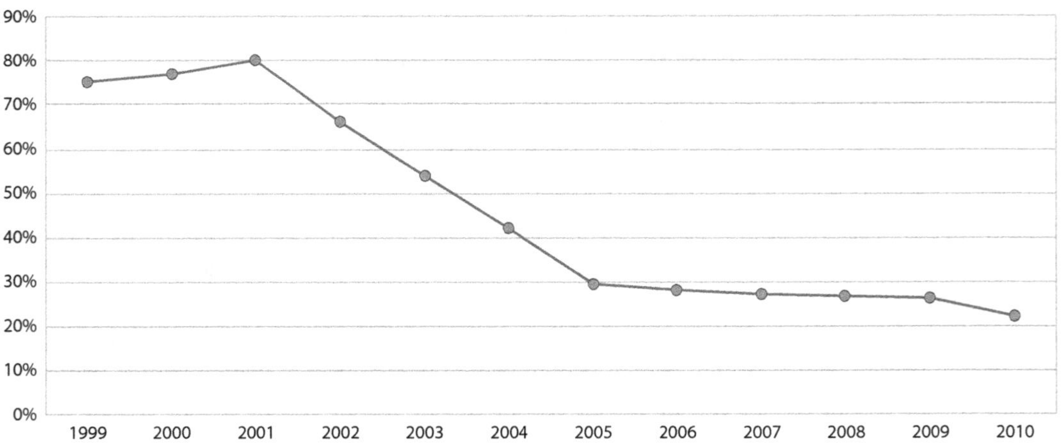

Source: Index Mundi, www.indexmundi.com/g/g.aspx?c=md&v=69.

This group (roughly the lowest income quintile) will have difficulty paying for anything. Because poverty is so widespread in Moldova, it makes more sense to focus exclusively on that lowest income quintile and discriminate only between the non-poor (i.e. those that can afford) and the poor (i.e. those that cannot afford). Therefore, this study focuses on the poorest income quintile.

Average expenses in Moldova for WSS as a percentage of income are at just below 3% (IBNET, 2014). As a result, the lowest income quintile likely spends more than 6% of its income on WSS.

More recent household survey data show that poverty has been gradually decreasing. However, the study focuses on a share lower than the mentioned quintile for the following reasons:

- The decrease in poverty cannot clearly be attributed to structural changes in the economy.
- Poverty may jump up again under adverse general economic developments as it has jumped down in recent years.
- Agriculture remains a main source of income for the lower income rural population. Adverse price developments can suddenly push people back into poverty.
- According to international institutions monitoring poverty, it is unclear how poverty has developed over recent years as data have not been published.

Nevertheless, the downward trend in poverty ratios is encouraging. Also, the household survey data contained important information with respect to the future design of WSS-related social measures. This is the subject of the next subsection, which touches on subjects that are discussed further in this and the next chapter.

Household surveys

Household survey data that use expenditure rather than income as the denominator show a larger share of expenses for WSS in total household (HH) expenditures (Figure 4.3 and Chapter 1).

Figure 4.3. **Percentage of total household expenditure spent on WSS in Moldova, by deciles**

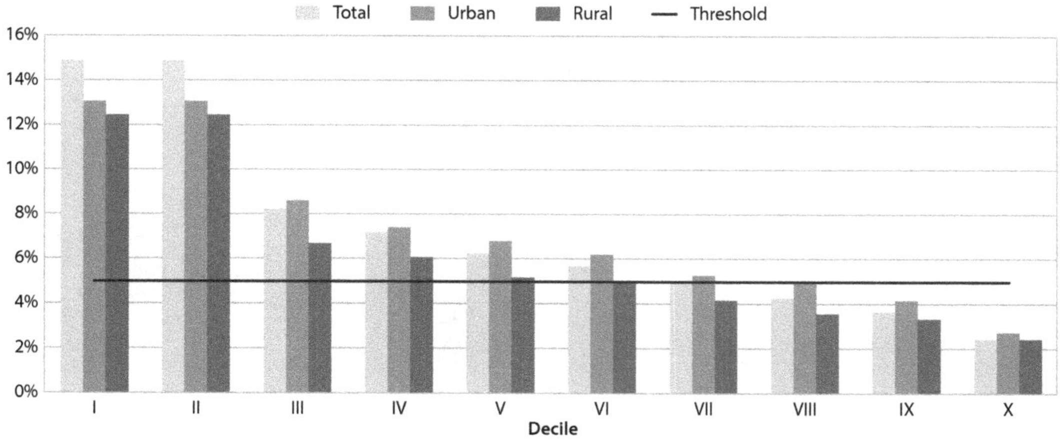

Source: Government of Moldova, WSS Strategy for 2014-28, http://lex.justice.md/ru/352311/.

Figure 4.3 illustrates or raises a number of critical issues:

- At 5% of average income, the average tariffs remain affordable for the average household. Considering the relatively low income of Moldova, the threshold may be set at this high level because lower income households spend more of their income on WSS. There is, however, little room to further increase average tariffs. This means efficiency increases and restructuring will need to be applied to keep water services generally affordable.
- The lowest (and even some mid-size) income deciles will hardly be able to spend more on WSS given the percentage of income they are spending currently on WSS (some more than 7%). This underlines the need for targeted social measures, rather than general measures with respect to tariffs.
- The Ministry of Economy (2014) reports that 13% of the population in Moldova lives in poverty. Poverty is concentrated in the lowest income decile and in rural areas. Currently, 84% of the poor lives in villages.
- The urban population spends a greater percentage on WSS than the rural population. Likely this has to do with access to drinking water services and the quality of the service. For all deciles, the urban population can spend more of its income on WSS than the rural population. Improved services will change the figure as even the poor rural population may be willing to take more and better quality WSS. Where there is no service one cannot spend money on it; however, one has to spend substantial funds for alternative water supply sources such as shallow wells or bottled water; see OECD (2007).
- The urban poor population is a much smaller group. The urban poor can be supported with targeted assistance given its small percentage: 1.0% in major cities, 2.4% in Chisinau region and 9.1% in small cities.
- For the rural population, the affordability of services will become critical once improved services become available. The challenge to provide for affordable services is bigger here. As noted in Figure 4.4, the share of rural population living in poverty is 18.8%. This is close to the maximum percentage that can be supported by cross-subsidies from households to households within a given service area. Therefore,

Figure 4.4. **Absolute poverty rates in different parts of Moldova**

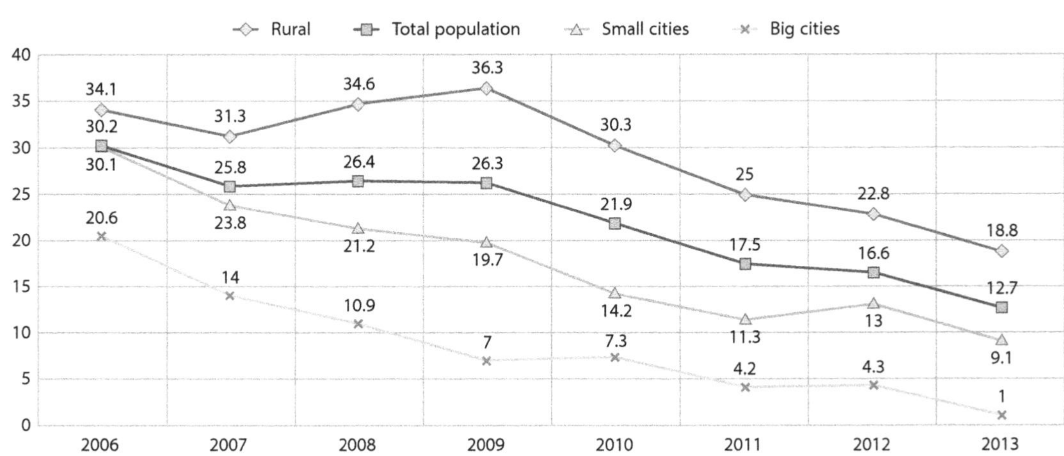

Source: Authors' elaboration based on BNS data.

regionalisation may be the only possibility. It will reduce the percentage of poverty in the expanded service area and hence make it easier to establish a cross-subsidy mechanism benefiting poorer (rural) households over richer (urban) households. Regionalisation of services does not eliminate or reduce regional differences in poverty rates across the country. As illustrated in Figure 4.4, incomes are converging. Affordability of service in one region will remain more of an issue in the south and the centre than in the north and Chisinau region.

- Figure 4.3 does not show that household tariffs vary widely from municipality to municipality. Regionalisation may change this as tariffs may become more uniform or harmonised. It is therefore important to develop "quick and easy to implement" social measures. Together with the evolving sector structure strategy, a more comprehensive social support mechanism should be developed. This will consider both geographic income distribution in Moldova, as well as income distribution within an (expanded) service area.

Through regionalisation, tariffs would become more harmonised. At that moment, the income and geographic-specific challenges can be addressed more comprehensively than through the "quick and easy to implement" measures.

4.3. Types of social support

Building on the financial flows described in previous chapters, existing domestic social support systems in Moldova are presented in Table 4.1. These systems represent those that aim to support affordability of, and access to, WSS in Moldova, among other objectives.

Table 4.1. **Identified domestic financial and social support systems in Moldova**

	Social support system	Effect	Form
I. Supply-related measures	Capital expenditure subsidy	Lowering capital expenditure costs of a WSS provider	Grant or in-kind donation from local or national government agency
II. Tariff-related measures	Operating expenditure subsidy	Reducing the discrepancy between operating income and operating expenditure of a WSS provider	Grant or in-kind donation from local or national government
	Indirect support	Allowing for continuation of services from WSS provider to vulnerable customers who do not pay fully or on time	Formal or informal measures that ease access to, or costs of, WSS, such as disconnection policies, lifelines, entitlements
	Cross-subsidies	WSS provider invoices below cost recovery level for that WSS	Cross-subsidies between municipal services, between WSS customer groups and between household customers
III. Income-related measures	Water-related income support	Improving income situation of WSS clients to pay their bills	National or local social benefits, earmarked for water-related expenses

Source: Based on authors' own findings.

The next chapter will outline a comprehensive framework for analysing and comparing WSS-related social measures that distinguishes three social support systems in the following areas:

- increasing the WSS connection rates (physical access)
- tariff-related measures
- income support measures.

Underneath each type of social measure may be one or more different, sometimes overlapping, measures with a WSS-related social impact. These measures may be carried out by one or more responsible organisations under one or more different programmes. For instance, both the NEF and the NFRD provide capital expenditure subsidies.

The following subsections assess social effectiveness and efficiency of the domestic demand-side and supply-side support mechanisms.

4.3.1. Supply-related measures

Measure 1: Capital expenditure subsidy

The National and Local Environmental Funds and the NFRD both described in Chapter 3 are the dominant sources of domestically financed capital expenditure. Neither of these funds has a primary objective in supporting identified social cases, but the NFRD aims to increase access to WSS.

Effectiveness of the instrument:

Capital expenditure costs are shared by all customers and/or taxpayers. Supporting capital expenditure is therefore not necessarily to the benefit of poor customers. However, if a particular capital expenditure subsidy expands the network, those previously not connected will benefit directly. Quite often these are more remote or rural areas. Hence, its effectiveness is valued at 80%. This value will be used later in a comparison table.

Size:

The size of the capital expenditure in network extension financed from domestic sources had to be estimated. The various budget lines sometimes combine capital expenditure for WSS with irrigation and other purposes. Optimistically, an estimated EUR 3.5 million from domestic sources is used for capital expenditure leading to network extension and improvement, particularly for the poor. That is in the order of around a euro per capita per year. Per capita consumption of 133 litres per capita per day (lcd) or 48 m^3 USD 1.12 average revenue per cubic metre per year translates to about EUR 0.02/m^3 (IBNET, 2014).

Evidence from projects indicates consumption in rural areas to be 50 lcd and in urban areas up to 100 lcd. On the other hand, not all capital expenditure is used for network expansion. Therefore, one can stick to an admittedly very rough estimate of EUR 0.02/m^3.

The translation of the support size to per cubic metre amounts is necessary for the comparison later on in this chapter.

Efficiency:

Table 4.2 indicates that access to improved water sources and sanitation – one of the Millennium Development Goals (MDGs) for 2015 – was already high by 2010.

Table 4.2. **MDGs in Moldova**

Indicator	2010
Access to improved water sources 2010 (%)	99
Access to improved sanitation 2010 (%)	89

Source: IBNET (2014), *The IBNET Water Supply and Sanitation Blue Book 2014*, www.IBNET.org, based on UNICEF and WHO (2012), *Progress on Drinking Water and Sanitation: 2012 Update*.

Based on these data, one may even question how capital expenditure can be increasing access to drinking water for the poor effectively. The data are quite inconsistent with the government of Moldova's data (UNDP, 2013). Table 4.3 provides data from the Third MDG Report.

Table 4.3. **Connection rates reported by Government of Moldova (2013)**

	2006	2007	2008	2009	2010	2010 target	2011	2012	2015 target
Share of population with permanent access to improved water sources, %	46	47	53	55	57	59	59	62	65
Population with access to improved sewage, %	43	44	46	48	51	50	55	57	65

Source: Government of Moldova (2013), *Report of the National Bureau of Statistics and the National Centre for Public Health.*

Table 4.4 shows connection rates of the 39 urban WSS providers for drinking water and sewerage in their service areas.

Table 4.4. **Connection rates reported by urban operators**

Moldova	2009	2010	2011	2012	2013
1.1 Water coverage (%)	80	80	83	84	81
2.1 Sewerage coverage (%)	65	67	69	70	67

Source: IBNET (2014), *The IBNET Water Supply and Sanitation Blue Book 2014*, www.IBNET.org.

The apparent inconsistency between the above tables is explained by these facts:

- Access to springs and shallow wells implies access to improved water sources. Water coverage as reported by the operators includes the percentage of households connected to a centralised (piped) water system.
- Access to improved sanitation also includes the availability of pit latrines.

The picture is complemented with further information in Tables 4.5 and 4.6 below.

Table 4.5. **WSS supply development**

	2009	2012
Publicly owned water supply systems		571
Total water supply systems	644	742
Of which operational	562	677
Sanitation systems	172	158
Of which operational		110
Of which WWTP		124

Source: Authors' findings based on MOE data.

Table 4.6. **WSS coverage in urban and rural areas**

	Urban areas	Rural areas
Coverage with centralised (piped) water supply systems	77%	36%
Centralised sanitation coverage	50%	1%

Source: data received through interview with Ms Tronza, MOE.

The number of operational water supply systems has significantly increased, while the number of operational sanitation systems has declined. There are insufficient data to assert that capital expenditure subsidies have not improved connection rates in Moldova, especially in rural areas. The government of Moldova (UNDP, 2013) reports consistent progress over the years. From other sources, such progress is not evident. It is not clear to what extent capital subsidies have been spent on network expansion compared to rehabilitating of existing systems. Furthermore, stakeholders have expressed hesitation with respect to the efficiency of how the two dedicated funds have been used. The efficiency has therefore been conservatively valued at (only) 60%. Improved data availability and consistency may require revision of this appraisal.

4.3.2 Tariff-related measures

Measure 2: Operating expenditure subsidy

Description:

Covering losses that relate to tariffs below cost recovery or to revenue collection rates well below 100% can be seen as a social support measure. Table 4.6 showed that many WSS utilities in Moldova do rely on operating subsidies or other forms of financial assistance from their owners i.e. the municipalities. These subsidies may amount to 8% of sales even though, legally speaking, they may be considered advances or capital increases rather than subsidies. Economically speaking, there is little doubt these are *de facto* subsidies.

Effectiveness of the instrument:

Operating subsidies are provided if a given tariff schedule cannot be adjusted because of political or social reasons. Existing tariffs in Moldova are typically uniform across households. Therefore, in absolute terms, those that consume the most water are the biggest beneficiaries of operational subsidies. Perversely, those consumers may be the ones who are better off. To be certain would require knowing the income elasticity of water demand in Moldova. There will certainly be a positive correlation between water demand and income, but the extent and strength of this relationship is unknown. Therefore, the benefit from operating subsidies accrues disproportionally to better off customers.

Despite the social connotation of the instrument, operating subsidies are not an effective way to target poor customers. They are to be applied in a transitional context or in times of crises. In the case of Moldova, operating subsidies have become a permanent feature. The effectiveness thereof is optimistically valued at 20%, equal to the percentage living below the poverty line.

Size:

Based on Table 4.6, the amount of money involved is estimated at 8% of sales, or EUR 0.07/m^3.

Efficiency:

Subsidies may keep tariffs below cost recovery. There are, however, knock-on effects of subsidisation that must be taken into account. First, they reduce the incentive of the operator to "earn" revenues by providing good service. Second, the knowledge that a subsidy would compensate for weak financial performance may create a moral hazard with respect to cost control within the operator. Over the long term, subsidies therefore may become less efficient. This study values the efficiency at 80%.

Measure 3: Indirect support

Description:

A number of either formal or informal measures may be applied at the utility level to ease the burden for vulnerable groups. One formal measure, for example, is the tariff structure aiming at a reduction of expenses for the poor. Informal measures include forgiving debt, refraining from disconnecting customers or exempting payments. Apart from tariff structures, it is difficult to assess these measures, let alone quantify them. Some measures, such as debt forgiveness, also require some discretion on the side of the operator.

Effectiveness of the instrument:

Local implementation of most measures means they may well be effective and customised for the local setting. This may be stronger than the lack of transparency. For effectiveness, a value of 80% is assigned.

Size:

It is hard to quantify this support system since a variety of measures are associated with it. Perhaps the revenue collection rate is most effective as a proxy. As other measures, the revenue collection rate hints at the extent of payment delay. According to IBNET (2014), the revenue collection rate has been close to 100% for the last five years and the payment period has not increased. This suggests that indirect support does not affect these indicators or that it plays only a minor role as a social support system; it is estimated at EUR 0.02/m^3 invoiced.

Efficiency:

As with size and effectiveness, the efficiency of this support mechanism is hard to estimate. This study considers it somewhat subjectively, and perhaps too optimistically, 75% efficient.

Measure 4: Cross subsidisation

Description:

Cross-subsidies of services come in three forms.

The first form, cross subsidy of municipal services, is common for combined service providers, but typically water services subsidise non-water services. The 39 urban operators provide only water-related services. Therefore, this form of cross subsidy is considered almost non-existent as a social support mechanism in Moldova.

The second form is the cross subsidy from industry to household customers, which gets reflected in tariff schedules. According to IBNET (2014), the ratio of industrial tariffs over household tariffs has been well over 300% for the years 2010-12. The tariff schedules submitted by the 39 incorporated operators show a ratio of 2.7 with a minima below 1.6 (including Chisinau) and maxima well over 4. By far, most respondents in the survey believed households paid at least 50% less than industry for water. Survey results can be found as an annex.

The third type of cross subsidy is from households consuming larger amounts to households consuming smaller amounts. This form of cross subsidy does not exist in any of the utilities applying a single volumetric tariff. These are all but two operators in Moldova (see Box 4.2). The combined effect of these two utilities on overall consumption is too small to consider cross-subsidies among household customers as a significant social support system.

Effectiveness:

In the main mechanism observed i.e. transfers from industry to all households, the pro-poor element is very small. The effectiveness of this mechanism is valued at 20%, the same as operating subsidies. For the same reason, all household customers benefit, instead of only the poor.

Box 4.2. Application of increasing block tariffs in Moldova

The most common tariff structure in Moldova is the single volumetric tariff. The tariff is similar for all households, but a different single volumetric tariff is charged for different types of customers. Two exceptional tariff structures are found in Soroca and Cahul; both are border cities with a population of just below 40 000 people.

Tariff MDL/m³ at various consumption levels		Consumption bracket in m³/month		
Operator	Service	up to 2	From 3 to 5	From 5 onwards
Regia Apacanal Soroca	Water	10.90	15.25	15.25
Apacanal Cahul	Water	6.00	6.00	12.00
	Sanitation	3.00	3.00	5.50

Both cities apply a higher charge for units of consumption above certain thresholds and both structures are examples of Increasing Block Tariffs (IBTs). These structures allow customers to use minimal amounts in order to stay within a more attractively priced consumption bracket. However, large customers also benefit from the cheap first few cubic metres provided. IBTs are therefore subsidising all customers instead of only the poor. This may, however, provide an incentive to limit consumption.

Source: interviews with the Association of Moldova Apacanals (AMAC).

Size:

Charging industrial tariffs more than households is the only significant mechanism. As a conservative estimate, businesses provide 46% of revenues from customers as described in Chapter 2. If businesses pay three times more for water and the average revenue is USD 1.12/m³ (IBNET, 2014) this suggests a hefty EUR 0.27/m³ invoiced.

Efficiency:

The main mechanism is easy to administer and, in that sense, is efficient. Longer term, however, industrial consumers risk taking care of their own water supply or bypassing the discriminatory pricing in another way, e.g. by building their own boreholes or surface water intakes. This will further erode the revenue base of the operators. The 40% non-revenue water (NRW) reported to IBNET (2014) may be explained in part by the high prices that industrial customers pay (IBNET data for NRW are 10% higher than data used in Moldovan sources). Further investigation is needed to distinguish between commercial and technical losses in Moldova and the sources of commercial losses. For now, efficiency must be valued at 65%, which is lower than the operating subsidy (80%).

4.3.3 Income-related measures

Measure 5: Water-related income support

Description:

The social security system in Moldova is summarised in Box 4.2. Apart from this general income support, the study could not identify targeted income support aimed at paying the water bill. Such support may well exist at municipal level in certain places. There is no such kind of support at the national level.

Effectiveness:

Municipalities typically know their citizens and are aware of their needs. Locally provided water-related income support may therefore be an effective way to provide water services for the poor. It may be valued at 80%.

Size:

The study could not come across examples of water-related income support. The overall size of this mechanism will be small; the value of EUR 0.01/m^3 is likely still too high.

Efficiency:

Due to high local administration costs, this type of support may have limited efficiency. However, since the study could not identify examples, it is difficult to judge. It has been valued at 75%.

4.4. Perceptions regarding social support

In addition to the inventory of existing social support systems, the project has surveyed attitudes and perceptions with respect to WSS-related social support measures in Moldova. The survey has been carried out among operators, municipalities and national government representatives.

The survey supports the assessment of existing social measures and the viability of possible new ones. A summary of the outcomes is presented below. The group of 39 urban operators provided a response large enough to summarise; other respondents provided useful insights, but not in sufficient numbers to draw a statistical meaningful conclusion. The full survey results can be found in Annex 3.

4.4.1. Response from urban operators

The survey supports the statement that tariffs vary widely across the country. The highest household tariffs is more than three times higher than the lowest reported among respondents. On average, industrial consumers also pay over three times the tariff of households per cubic metre.

There are a few examples of the application of block tariffs in Moldova. Non-revenue water is reported at an average of just below 30%.

There is some agreement that the NEF should increase access to drinking water, and slightly more agreement that the NFRD should do so. Overall, support for improving access for the poor through these funds is not very strong. Some believe that locally provided investment subsidies (through the NEF) do support access.

The answers as to whether current systems can accommodate more complex tariff structures vary widely. There is some agreement that the economic regulator must consider the affordability of WSS and determine a favourable tariff regime for poorer households. Local operating subsidies are only faintly believed to be essential for service provision to the poor.

Social support systems also include measures such as offering or accepting late payment, ruling out disconnection and other forms of formal and informal assistance. The operators give inconclusive answers with respect to how well social cases have been identified and what policies support them. They do, however, agree strongly that some autonomy at the local level is a good way to address social issues. Operators do not see much solidarity among household customers within their service area. This limits the scope for any rebate or similar mechanism reducing the bill for social cases.

On the existence of various forms of cross-subsidies, the answers are also inconclusive. The exception is the cross subsidy from industry to households. Operators indicate households pay less than half of the industrial tariff.

Table 4.7. **Summary table: Responses of urban operators**

		Agree on scale 0-10 (10 means total agreement)	Average	Median	St Dev	No of respondents
Supply-related	Q5	Providing access to piped drinking water is much more important than supporting poor households that have access already.	6.8	8.0	2.6	19
Tariff-related	Q12	The economic regulator (ANRE) should determine a tariff mechanism that favours poorer households.	8.0	8.0	2.2	20
Income-related	Q15	The fee collector has the skills and autonomy to deal with customers that cannot afford paying the bill.	4.8	5.5	3.4	20
Other	Q19	Only a regional operator has the capacity to implement a social tariff policy.	5.8	6.5	3.3	20
	Q20	Customers understand that in one way or another they need to pay a bit more for their water in order to support poorer households.	4.0	3.5	3.3	20

Note: **St Dev**: standard deviation; **Q**: "question" (referring to its number in the questionnaire sent out to Apacanals during the limited survey).

Source: Authors' findings based on survey feedback from Apacanals.

Table 4.8. **Summary table: Responses of village operators**

		Agree on scale 0-10 (10 means total agreement)	Average	Median	St Dev	No of respondents
Supply-related	Q5	Providing access to piped drinking water is much more important than supporting poor households that have access already.	6.6	8.0	3.7	5
Tariff-related	Q12	The economic regulator (ANRE) should determine a tariff mechanism that favours poorer households.	7.8	8.0	1.5	5
Income-related	Q15	The fee collector has the skills and autonomy to deal with customers that cannot afford paying the bill.	8.3	9.5	2.9	4
Other	Q19	Only a regional operator has the capacity to implement a social tariff policy.	9.3	10.0	1.5	4
	Q20	Customers understand that in one way or another they need to pay a bit more for their water in order to support poorer households.	4.0	4.0	3.7	4

Note: **St Dev**: standard deviation; **Q**: "question" (referring to its number in the questionnaire sent out to Apacanals during the limited survey).

Source: Authors' findings based on survey feedback from Apacanals.

4.5. Comparing domestic social support systems

Taking into account the observations above and the survey results, is it possible to evaluate the existing social support systems in Moldova against one another? A comprehensive evaluation would certainly require more study.

The study has made rough estimates regarding size, effectiveness and efficiency of the identified social support systems based on observations, interviews with stakeholders, previous and own analysis of the subject. The study considers these estimates "roughly correct" as opposed to "precisely wrong". Table 4.9 shows these estimates provide a sufficient basis for the evaluation because of the outspoken outcomes.

Stakeholders are invited to put forward their own evaluation. Through dialogue and further investigation, a consensus can emerge on next steps.

It is estimated that the largest amount of money spent with a social objective is the cross subsidy from industry to household. At the same time, this instrument provides the least value for money i.e. it is assisting the poor neither effectively nor efficiently.

The second type of social measure in terms of size is operating subsidies, which also provide low value for money. However, they consume significant financial resources that cannot be used for other, more effective social measures.

The three social support systems that perform relatively well – capital expenditure subsidies, indirect support and WSS-related income support – are all much smaller. As noted earlier, these measures may perform much better, but few domestic resources are spent on them in Moldova.

Comparing social support measures is like comparing apples and oranges. There are also insufficient data readily available for a study like the current one. There is, however, a strong difference in performance of the measures; major resources are spent on the badly performing measures.

Moldova cannot afford a waste of resources in a way that some Western European countries can.

As a minimum, Table 4.9 below illustrates:

- the need to rethink the provision of water-related social support
- the need for an integrated approach towards the design of alternatives
- the need to put the primary beneficiary of these measures in the centre (i.e. the lowest income quintile).

Table 4.9. **Evaluation of relative importance of identified social support systems**

	Quantification of support mechanisms	A. Pro poor element (Effectiveness)	B. Monetary amount involved (Size)	C. Efficiency of delivery	D. Result (A*B*C)	E. Normalised result	F. Value for money (E/B)
1	Capital expenditure subsidy	80%	0.02	60%	0.010	14%	7.1
2	Operational expenditure subsidy	20%	0.07	80%	0.011	17%	2.4
3	Indirect support	80%	0.02	75%	0.011	16%	8.9
4	Cross-subsidisation	20%	0.27	65%	0.036	53%	1.9
5	Water related income support measures	80%	0.01	80%	0.006	10%	9.5
		na	1.00	na	0.067	100%	na

Source: Authors' findings and estimates.

Explanations:

A. This column estimates the percentage of beneficiaries in the lowest income quintile based on various facts and observations.

B. This column expresses the annual cost of the instrument per cubic metre of water invoiced in Moldova, recalculated in euros. Expressing the amount in per cubic metre terms allows for a better comparison across various social instruments.

C. The efficiency of delivery considers the cost of administering the mechanism in relation to the social goal to be achieved. Capital expenditure subsidy has been given a low efficiency because it is not targeted at increasing the connection ratio. It does not imply that it is inefficient or unwise to provide these subsidies, but as a social support mechanism it is less efficient. At the same time, it may be a very efficient way to improve health, environment or general income development.

D. This is the product of the previous three columns and indicates the absolute social impact of the instrument expressed in per cubic metres.

E. The normalised results is the same indicator, but shows better the relative impact using percentages adding up to 100%.

F. The amount of money spent for a certain effect is indicated in the final column by dividing the result by column B again. A similar relative ranking can be obtained by multiplying items in column A and C. Efficiency and effectiveness indicate as well how much "value for money" the instrument generates.

4.6. Conclusion

Water-related social support systems in Moldova are underdeveloped. Given the size of the population living below the official poverty line, there is very little available in terms of discount, hardship relief or support to become connected to the system.

Existing delivery mechanisms suffer from:

- lack of a specific focus on the poor (e.g. capital expenditure projects also have economic and environmental targets)
- ineffectiveness of the support mechanism (e.g. low tariffs benefit rich and poor customers alike)
- inefficient delivery of the support mechanism (e.g. it is not clear if subsidies keep tariffs low or rather sustain cost-inefficient delivery of service and overstaffing).

Different stakeholders have their own interests and perspectives. For instance, utilities have an interest in sustainability of operations. Customers have an interest in low tariffs for everyone. The economic regulator has focused more on cost recovery, so far without special attention for the poor.

While this is understandable and logical, consistent and efficient water-related social measures are needed. In the present institutional context in the WSS, there is little attention for the poorest 20% of the population. It is therefore important to look both for **water-related social measures,** as well as for **institutional structures** that will warrant the interest of the very poor. The next chapter looks at both for a selected group of four reference countries.

References

Government of Moldova (2014), *WSS Strategy for 2014-28,* http://lex.justice.md/ru/352311/

Government of Moldova (2013), *Report of the National Bureau of Statistics and the National Centre for Public Health.*

IBNET (2014), *The IBNET Water Supply and Sanitation Blue Book 2014*, The International, Benchmarking Network for Water and Sanitation Utilities Databook/World Bank, Washington, DC, www.IBNET.org, accessed 28 September 2014.

Index Mundi, www.indexmundi.com/g/g.aspx?c=md&v=69.

UNDP (2013), *The third national report on Millennium Development Goals in Moldova: Progress achieved, remaining issues and future options*, 24 September 2013, United Nations Development Programme, www.md.undp.org/content/moldova/en/home/presscenter/pressreleases/.

UNICEF and WHO (2012), *Progress on Drinking Water and Sanitation: 2012 Update*, Joint Monitoring Programme for Water Supply and Sanitation, United Nations Children's Fund, New York; World Health Organization, Geneva, www.unicef.org/media/files/JMPreport2012.pdf.

World Bank (2014), *Enhanced social safety nets for Moldova's poorest households*, www.worldbank.org/en/results/2014/04/15/enhanced-social-safety-nets-for-moldovas-poorest-households.

World Bank (2013), *Water sector regionalisation review, Republic of Moldova*, World Bank, Washington, DC.

Chapter 5

Social support systems in reference countries

This chapter briefly overviews social support systems related to water supply and sanitation in four reference countries: Armenia, France, Romania and Ukraine, and draws some lessons from their experience relevant for Moldova.

To have a better understanding of the options for Moldova, the social measures related to water supply and sanitation (WSS) in a number of countries have been analysed. Four of these countries were chosen as reference countries: Armenia, France, Romania and Ukraine. Each reference country experience is relevant for Moldova, but also has its limitations; occasionally, reference is made to non-reference countries to explain examples of particular social support systems. What binds all the reference countries and Moldova together is subscription to the principles of the **EU Water Framework Directive (WFD).** This requires, apart from the often mentioned application of the full cost recovery and polluter pays principles, the availability of a minimum of water to all at an affordable price. To apply that latter principle, countries have a variety of social measures at their disposal.

5.1. Social support system categorisation and inventory

For analysis of social support systems in the reference countries, the analytical framework provided by OECD (2002, 49) was used (see Figure 5.1). The following should be taken into account to apply this framework for this study:

- Unlike transition countries, most OECD member countries have connection ratios close to their economic maximum. Yet, for transition countries, increasing connection rates to piped water networks must be considered as a possible social measure, too. This is because positive social effects are so vast on health, income generation, time and cost savings (energy, bottled water). The nature of the spending is different. Investment in increased coverage by piped WSS is, in fact, a social investment, rather than a social expense.
- The meaning of "social" has been interpreted narrowly i.e. it does not include intergenerational solidarity. Incomplete cost recovery is therefore defined as a possible social measure because it allows for lower tariffs. Not recovering the full environmental and resource costs is also defined as a social measure for the same reason, although it may not be particularly social towards future generations.
- Pricing in the ecological needs for water conservation and wastewater treatment is certainly "social", particularly towards next generations. This study, however, considers only the current generation.
- Underneath the term "cross-subsidies" are three distinctly different mechanisms, each of which must be considered individually as discussed in 5.2.2.
- Preferential VAT rates are considered as a tariff-related measure because – from the end user perspective – it affects affordability of service directly.
- Rebates and discounts can come either as a tariff-related measure directly, or indirectly as an income support measure.

For this study, therefore, the analytical framework has been extended and customised (Table 5.1). Based on this analytical framework, an inventory was made of which social support systems are applied in which country. However, social support measures may be changing over time, be offsetting other aspects of the social system and applied differently, also within one country. Therefore, each item of the inventory is explained for each individual sub-item. Towards the end of the chapter, there is a conclusion for each reference country and its relevance for Moldova. These will be taken into account in the development of scenarios for creating social support measures.

Figure 5.1. **Social support systems OECD analytical framework**

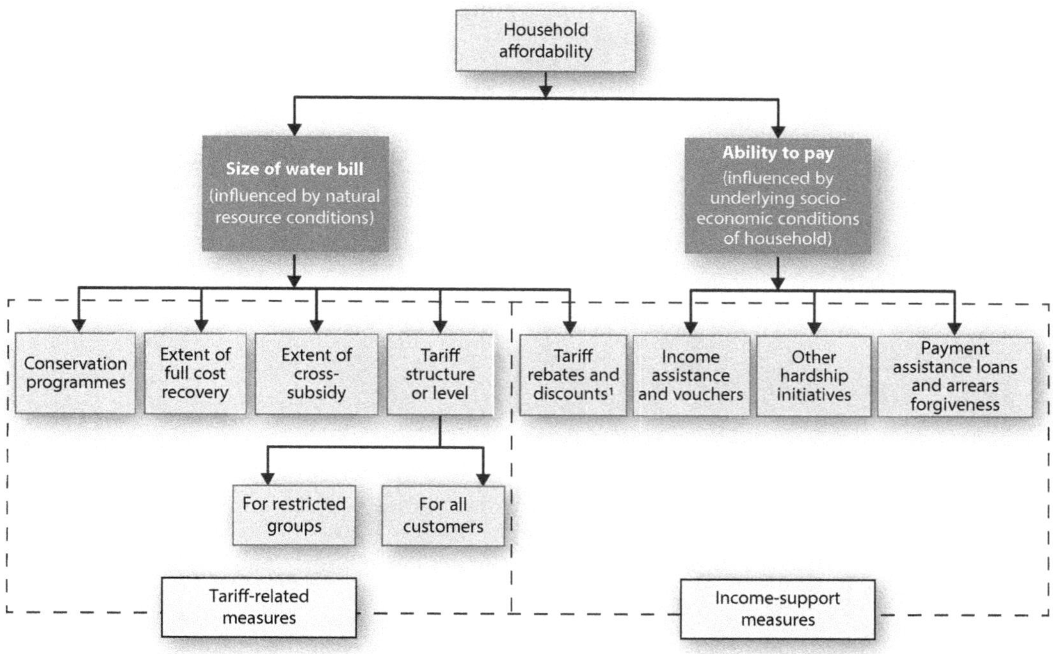

Source: OECD (2002), *Social Issues in the Provision and Pricing of Water Services.*

Figure 5.2. **Social support systems, extended analytical framework for transition context**

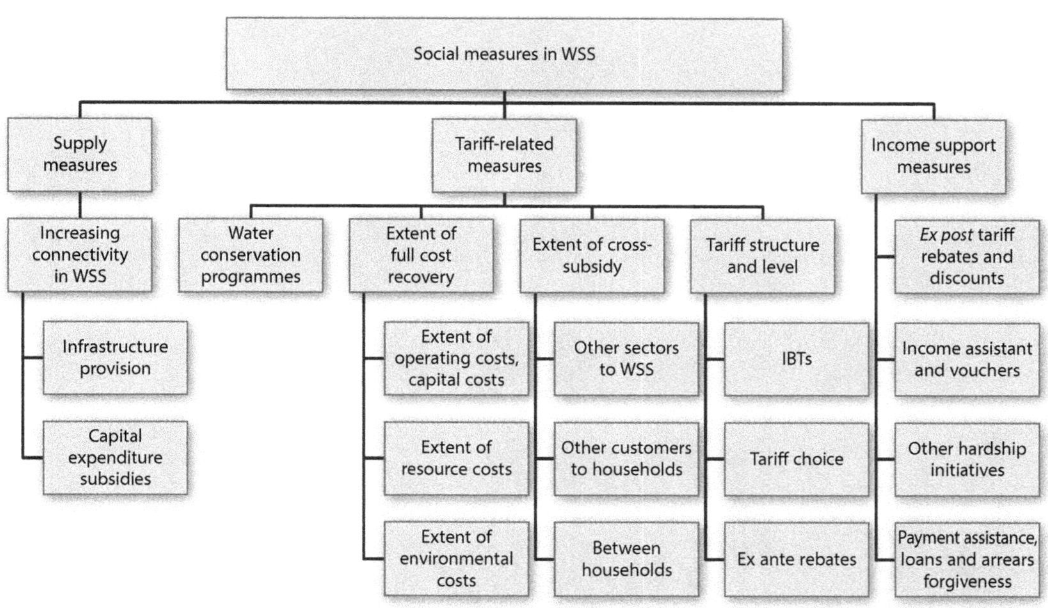

Source: Authors' own elaboration based on OECD (2002), *Social Issues in the Provision and Pricing of Water Services.*

Table 5.1. **Inventory of social support systems in Moldova and reference countries**

Social support system	Moldova	Armenia	France	Romania	Ukraine
I. Supply measures					
I.1 Increasing connection rates (coverage) for WSS (through capital expenditure subsidy)	++	++	++	+++	+++
II. Tariff-related measures					
II.1 Conservation programmes for poor (including leakage reduction) (such as in United States, Australia)	◊	◊	+	◊	◊
II.2 Reduced extent of full cost recovery (i.e. including environmental and resource costs)					
II.2.1 Reduced recovery of operating costs (including depreciation) and costs of capital	+++	+++		++	+++
II.2.2 Reduced consideration of resource costs	+++	+++	+	+++	+++
II.2.3 Reduced consideration of environmental costs	+++	+++	+	+++	+++
II.3 Extent of cross subsidy					
II.3.1 From other sectors to WSS	+	-	-	-	-
II.3.2 From business and institutions to households	+++	+++	-	+++	+++
II.3.3 From higher income households to lower income households	+	-	++	-	+
II.4 Tariff structure or level					
II.4.1 Tariff structure	+	-	-	-	-
II.4.2 Tariff choice	-	-	-	-	-
II.4.3 Exemptions, *ex ante* rebates and discounts	◊	-	-	◊	+++
III. Income support measures					
III.1 *Ex post* tariff rebates and discounts	-	-	-	◊	+++
III.2 Income assistance and vouchers	-	-	+	◊	-
III.3 Other hardship initiatives	◊	◊	+++	◊	◊
IV.4 Payment assistance, loans and arrear forgiveness	◊	◊	+++	◊	◊

Legend: ◊ Could not be identified

- Does not exist in this country

\+ Does exist but plays a rather symbolic role as a social support measure

++ Does exist but plays a relatively unimportant role as a social support measure

+++ Does exist and does plays an important role as a social support measure

Source: Authors' own assessment.

5.2. Elaboration on the inventory

5.2.1. Supply measures

Table 5.2 evaluates whether supply measures are used as a tool of social policy through development of access to drinking water and sanitation.

Table 5.2. **WSS in reference countries**

Moldova	**2009**	**2010**	**2011**	**2012**	**2013**
1.1 Water Coverage (%)	80	80	83	84	81
2.1 Sewerage Coverage (%)	65	67	69	70	67
Armenia	**2006**	**2007**	**2008**	**2009**	**2010**
1.1 Water Coverage (%)	79	80	80	90	91
2.1 Sewerage Coverage (%)	35	34	35	37	37
Romania	**2006**	**2007**	**2008**	**2009**	**2010**
1.1 Water Coverage (%)	87	87	84	82	84
2.1 Sewerage Coverage (%)	74	74	69	65	62
Ukraine	**2003**	**2004**	**2005**	**2006**	**2007**
1.1 Water Coverage (%)	93	94	78	79	80
2.1 Sewerage Coverage (%)	69	69	63	64	67
France	**2003**	**2004**	**2005**	**2006**	**2007**
1.1 Water Coverage (%)					99
2.1 Sewerage Coverage (%)					80

Source: IBNET (2014), *The IBNET Water Supply and Sanitation Blue Book 2014*, Barraqué and Le Bris,(2007), *Water Sector Regulation in France.*

Table 5.2 must be carefully interpreted as IBNET contains data on relatively large operators that operate mostly in urban areas; coverage by piped WSS services in rural areas might be much lower (e.g. in Moldova only 1% of rural population has connection to piped/ centralised sanitation).

With connection rates at 99.5% for water and 80% for sanitation, there is no social policy purpose for increasing coverage in France. For supporting construction of infrastructure in rural areas, there is a 1% solidarity tax on the water bill. The proceeds of this tax have been instrumental in raising the connection rates in France up to their current levels.

All three other reference countries still need to raise connection rates. In Armenia, according to IBNET (2014), the sanitation coverage is extremely low at just over 35%. The Medium Term Expenditure Framework for Armenia, however, reports a coverage ratio of 63%. However, this regards only the five main operators, operating mostly in urban settlements and in villages close to cities. National investment strategies foresee a strong need for investment, also using domestic resources. In urban water supply, coverage increased from 71-91% between 2006-10. Only a fraction may have been financed domestically, but there is a clear priority towards increasing access to WSS.

Romania spends 45% of the EU Cohesion Fund allocations on environment (including water, in particular). Considering a co-financing ratio of at least 10%; this means the country is using domestic resources for improving water supply and increasing coverage in the order of EUR 100 million annually (European Commission, 2009). This suggests raising connectivity is an important social measure.

Ukraine's commitment to increasing connection rates is less clear cut. On the one hand, there was a budgetary commitment towards improving water supply in 2011 and 2012 in the order of EUR 10 million (Ukrainian Pilot Project Team of the UNECE [2013]).

But at most only a fraction was earmarked for increasing connection rates; the actual disbursements for projects have been reported as less than 20% of the committed amounts.

Furthermore, connection rates are currently not monitored and progress cannot be measured. The latest available data in IBNET (2014) date back to 2007. These show a connection rate of 80% for drinking water and 67% for sanitation services. The years before 2007 show only slightly lower percentages for sanitation. At least since 2008, the Danube programme has started trying to improve performance monitoring, but these have yet to bear fruit (WB & IADB, 2014). The most recent available information is provided in Table 5.3.

Table 5.3. **Access to centralised (piped) drinking water and sanitation systems in Ukraine**

Area	Drinking water		Sanitation
	2008	2010	
Urban	88%	91%	Urban
Rural	28%	26%	Rural

Source: interview with the State Water Resources Agency of Ukraine.

This table suggests progress on access to drinking water in urban areas in particular, compared to the earlier 2007 data. However, the Ukrainian Pilot Project Team of the UNECE (2013) reports that no active policy is aimed at increasing the coverage by centralised WSS, that data are unreliable and hard to get, and that policies were aimed at avoiding a collapse of drinking water systems rather than on their expansion. Therefore, increasing access to WSS cannot yet be considered a strong priority in Ukrainian social policy.

For comparison, the previous chapter described increasing connection rates as a social measure in Moldova. It concluded that domestic resources spent on increasing connection rates amounted to a few million euros annually, but were hard to distinguish from other measures.

5.2.2. Tariff-related measures

Gradual introduction of commercial tariffs contributes to more a sustainable WSS system. However, it also introduces additional challenges, especially in transition countries with specific attitude towards access to public utilities, high costs of WSS services driven by inefficiency of WSS systems that are often highly deteriorated and/or oversized, and the roles of governments in the sector's sustainability and development. Many governments tend to mitigate the risks on access and affordability by introducing some direct and indirect social support mechanisms, either directly related to WSS or through more universal approaches. This section discusses the existing practices of WSS-related direct and indirect support to socially vulnerable households, including tariff-related measures. Each time reference to measures listed in Table 5.1 is made.

Conservation programmes for poor (including leakage reduction) – measure II.1 in Table 5.1

Reducing the water bill by consuming less water is an economically and environmentally sound strategy, assuming that consumption does not fall below a certain minimum absolutely necessary for human beings. Poorer customers often live in houses and apartment blocks in which the plumbing is of lower quality. In the United States and Australia, there are examples of programmes targeting poorer neighbourhoods (OECD, 2002). No such examples have been identified in any of the reference countries or Moldova. If they exist, they are set up as environmental programmes rather than social policy measures. In France, the introduction of metering was accompanied by awareness campaigns. But these campaigns targeted the political acceptability of metering and should not be considered as a form of social support system.

Reduced extent of full cost recovery (i.e. including environmental and resource costs) – measure II.2

Tariffs can be kept lower if operators effectively need not or may not recover all the costs incurred. All customers benefit from "lower than should be" tariffs. The net benefit for customers may be positive or negative, taking into account delayed maintenance, repair and replacement.

Larger consumers gain the most from lower tariffs as they consume more units at a lower price than small consumers. Future generations clearly do not benefit from this "social measure" as the price for repair and renewal must eventually be paid. That price will be on their shoulders.

People without any access to WSS do not benefit from lower tariffs. Suppressed tariffs decrease the likelihood of their connection in the future as they erode the business case for network expansion.

Yet, despite the lack of targeting the ones who need it, below cost recovery tariffs are widely perceived as a legitimate part of the social policy mix.

Reduced recovery of operating costs (including depreciation) and capital costs – measure II.2.1

Human resource and variable costs such as electricity and chemicals must be recovered in order to avoid acute cash flow problems or ever-accumulating accounts payables. This is not the case for some other cost items. Depreciation expenses, for example, can be kept artificially low by avoiding capitalisation of assets, a common phenomenon in Eastern Europe and Central Region (EECCA) countries. Opaque ownership structures and accounting standards not consistent with International Financial Reporting Standards enable the use of assets without depreciating them on the balance sheet. Costs are therefore recovered on paper, but no funds for renewal and replacement are built up. Adding this to insufficient maintenance is degradation of respective WSS systems by the mid-term of their life cycles (Zetland, 2014).

Because depreciation is not a cash expense, its under-recovery does not pose an immediate threat to operations. Longer term sustainability of the operations is eroded unless the government provides for replacement and renewal. This, however, builds in a systematic dependence on government that may have a political dimension. Funding for investment may be available only for political allies (e.g. for settlements where the majority votes for the respective political party).

The operating cost coverage ratio indicates how many times revenues cover operating costs before depreciation. Since the denominator excludes depreciation, a level of 1.3–1.5 could be considered as a minimum for longer term sustainability.

Operating costs coverage ratio in Ukraine was significantly below 1 until at least 2008, suggesting cash deficit and accumulating accounts payable.

Armenia and Romania are at a higher rate of cost recovery, but still insufficient to recover depreciation. IBNET data for France are not available. However Table 5.5 shows that France recovers operating costs, including depreciation and even debt service.

From the reference countries, only France applies tariffs sufficient to recover both operating costs (depreciation and capital costs). French utilities, hence, reinvest typically without external financing (or are able to do so).

Three of the four reference countries apply a policy of keeping tariffs below cost recovery, often against domestically adopted policies. The sums involved to carry out this

Table 5.4. **Financial and cost recovery ratios for reference countries**

Moldova	**2007**	**2008**	**2009**	**2011**	**2012**
Average revenue W&WW (USD/m³ water sold)	0.92	1.06	1.15	1.14	1.12
Collection period (days)	259	246	273	282	274
Collection ratio (percentage)	101	98	97	101	98
Operating cost coverage (ratio)	1.05	1.14	1.08	1.09	0.99
Armenia	**2009**	**2010**	**2011**	**2012**	**2013**
Average revenue W&WW (USD/m³ water sold)	0.29	0.41	0.47	0.44	0.47
Collection period (days)	455	236	266	296	281
Collection ratio (percentage)	72	83	87	79	80
Operating cost coverage (ratio)	0.88	1	1.05	0.98	0.98
Romania	**2006**	**2007**	**2008**	**2009**	**2010**
Average revenue W&WW (USD/m³ water sold)	0.78	1.08	1.2	1.08	1.02
Collection period (days)	97	85	80	80	87
Collection ratio (percentage)	106	104	107	108	112
Operating Cost Coverage (ratio)	1.24	1.18	1.07	1.1	1.08
Ukraine	**2003**	**2004**	**2005**	**2006**	**2007**
Average revenue W&WW (USD/m³ water sold)	0.19	0.22	0.25	0.32	0.44
Collection period (days)	399	361	278	251	225
Collection ratio (percentage)	75	85	92	84	92
Operating cost coverage (ratio)	0.91	0.96	0.84	0.87	0.91

Source: IBNET (2014), *The IBNET Water Supply and Sanitation Blue Book 2014.*

form of social policy are significant and in the order of 20-30% of the actual tariff. Part of the costs of this social policy will be paid for by future generations in the form of insufficient maintenance, shorter economic asset life and higher investment needs. As for Moldova, Table 5.4 shows that tariffs do not cover depreciation costs.

In **Armenia,** the central government rather than operators is responsible for funding capital expenditures. Depreciation is not a cost item of the tariff structure, but instead part of the financial statements of the operators' reporting according to international standards (IFRS). However, in some cases, depreciation is quite marginal as the historical price and book value of fixed assets older than 12-15 years have not been properly adjusted to the huge inflation accumulated since 1989. The book value of old fixed assets appropriated before 2000 is many times lower than their present replacement or even liquidation value.

Regulated tariffs are kept even below the level required to recuperate the operators' (reduced) operating costs, let alone the cost of capital. The law stipulates that operators can apply for an operational subsidy compensating for the shortfall in revenues, i.e. to cover the cash flow gap (OECD EAP Task Force, 2007). The full amount of subsidies and capital expenditure by the government must be considered as part of the social policy mix with respect to WSS. It must be evaluated against alternative social measures.

For a population of 3 million people, the amount of funds involved is significant – in the order of USD 20 million annually, or almost USD 7.00 per capita. A third is spent on subsidies compensating for the shortfall in revenues due to regulated prices. Considering a drinking water tariff in the order of USD 0.50/m^3, one can estimate the extent of resources spent for social measures.

In **Ukraine,** tariffs must be set on the basis of cost plus necessary investments. If local authorities approve tariffs insufficient to cover these economic costs, then they must compensate for the revenue shortfall through a subsidy (Ukrainian Pilot Project Team of the UNECE [2013, 26]). The 2012 national budget, however, planned EUR 400 million to reimburse local authorities for debt to service providers resulting from tariffs below economic costs. This is also a significant amount for a population of 44 million. Although the tariff should consider necessary investments, the 2012 budget also reserves an earlier mentioned EUR 10 million for investment in the sector. Both amounts must be seen as social measures to keep tariffs below cost recovery.

Romania does not entitle operators to compensation in the way that other reference countries do. Municipalities mostly refrain from subsidising operators, even though tariffs do not always recover economic costs.

As mentioned above, **France** does not need to provide subsidies as it applies the principle of "*L'eau paie l'eau*" ("water pays for water").

Table 5.5. **Cost coverage ratio for domestic water supply and sanitation services in selected OECD member countries, OECD survey results, 2008**

Country	Ratio	Comments
Belgium:		Most likely includes debt service and depreciation
Brussels	1.05	
Wallonia	1.11	
France	1.0	Most likely includes debt service and depreciation
Sweden	1.0	
Northern Ireland	1.0	

Source: OECD (2010), *Pricing Water Resources and Sanitation Services.*

If billing to consumers is insufficient to recover the sum of operating costs (including depreciation) and capital costs (costs of debt and equity), then an operator is operating below financial cost recovery. Allowing or forcing to operate below financial cost recovery is at best a transitional solution. As a social measure, it may keep tariffs low for a while. Without operating subsidies, fixed assets and WSS service quality begin gradually to decline. But operating subsidies themselves make service providers increasingly dependent and pave the way to a politicised environment. This process will have negative long-term effects on performance.

Box 5.1. **Reduced VAT rates as a social measure**

A lower value added tax (VAT) rate improves affordability of services without harming the operator directly. As water is considered an essential good, most EU countries apply a beneficial VAT rate for WSS services. This group includes Romania and Bulgaria. The national government bears the economic costs of this social measure, losing revenues it cannot apply for other social measures in WSS. As with lower WSS tariffs, the benefits of a lower VAT rate accrue to customers:

- that are already connected to WSS services
- in proportion to the amount of the service consumed

As with tariffs, the social measure of a reduced VAT rate is not well targeted. Poor customers would be better off with the establishment or financing of a WSS connection or more targeted support measures. For Armenia, it is estimated that only 11% of total benefits for lower household tariffs (including a lower VAT rate) goes to the poorest 20%. Such measures also take away the incentive to reduce drinking water consumption, which could be an alternative cost-saving mechanism for the poor.

Source: Authors' own opinion and observation.

France does not allow operating below financial cost recovery. Romania is in a transitional phase without subsidies, but tariffs occasionally fall short of financial cost recovery. In Armenia and Ukraine, subsidies are an institutionalised part of the system. The subsidy process in Armenia, however, is a lot more transparent and reliable than it is in Ukraine.

Reduced consideration of environmental and resource costs – measures II.2.2 and II.2.3

In addition to recovering operating costs (including depreciation) and capital costs, Article 9 of the Water Framework Directive (WFD) requires taking environmental and resource costs into account. Environmental costs represent the costs of damage that water use imposes on the environment and ecosystems. Resource costs are opportunity costs that other uses suffer due to the depletion of the resource beyond its natural rate of recharge or recovery. Defining and "pricing in" these costs into WSS services is a requirement for Member States such as France and Romania, but may guide policies also in Armenia and Ukraine.

Pricing in environmental and resource costs will not necessarily increase revenues for the operator. However, it will definitely increase the total water bill through the sum of tariffs (revenues for operators), taxes (collection of funds for government) or charges (collection of earmarked funds administered by government or agencies).

France and Romania have water abstraction charges and water consumption charges, as well as a sewage charge, water effluent charge and water pollution non-compliance fees. France has wastewater usage and water effluent charges, plus a general tax on pollution, as well as charges on water supply. Apart from the tax on pollution and noncompliance taxes, all the other charges are on top of the WSS bill.

In Armenia, however, environmental and resource costs are still in their infancy and play a marginal role in the overall bill (Ukrainian Pilot Project Team of the UNECE [2013]). For Ukraine, no reliable information on economic instruments could be found. Since tariffs are not even covering operating costs (including depreciation), it is unlikely there are substantial supplementary charges in either of these countries. Although environmental and resource costs are different from economic costs, full cost recovery is usually approached step by step. That means that countries will first strive to recover the financial and economic costs before addressing full cost recovery i.e. including environmental and resource costs. Institutional arrangements must be in place before economic instruments can be applied. Otherwise, it may result in monopoly rent or waste of financial resources collected in funds or through the government.

But the reasons for not charging for environmental and resource costs may also be social i.e. the fear for its effect on affordability of service. With the exception of France, the lack of full cost recovery must therefore be seen as a social measure in all reference

Table 5.6. **Prices, taxes and charges**

	On water abstraction	On water consumption	On wastewater discharges and treatment	On other
France	Charge on water abstraction	Charge on water supply Charge on water consumption	Wastewater user charges Water effluent charges	General tax on polluting activities
Romania	Water abstraction charge (groundwater and surface water)	Water consumption charge	Sewage charge. Effluent charge. Water pollution non-compliance fees	Fishing permits

Source: European Environment Agency (2013), *Assessment of Cost Recovery Through Water Pricing.*

countries. As with financial cost recovery, the benefits are spread over all customers and accrue only to a small extent to the poor. The cost of this "social support measure" will be mostly paid by future generations.

In Moldova, charges on water abstraction or pollution do not exist. Instead, the NEF benefits from environmental charges on packaging. As these charges are also used for projects in the water sector, the reduced consideration of environmental and resource costs is also a means to keep tariffs below full cost recovery in Moldova. As long as financial costs are not recovered, environmental and resource costs are often considered a secondary priority.

Extent of cross subsidisation – measure II.3

The concepts of full cost recovery and the polluter pays principle, which are so fundamental to the WFD, are inconsistent with cross subsidisation. Transfers between different types of household customers, however, are a special form of cross subsidy that may be allowed under

Article 9. EU Member States in particular need to replace cross-subsidies with alternative social support systems. EU accession countries that use the WFD as a guiding document should also consider phasing out cross-subsidies.

Cross-subsidies can be explicit in the form of transfers from one municipal service to another or of higher tariffs for certain customers and lower for others. They can also be implicit or hidden through improper allocation of costs or avoiding the use of cost centres altogether. Various cross-subsidies continue to play an important role as a social support system, also in EU Member States. This study does not consider cross-subsidies between water and wastewater services.

Cross-subsidies from other sectors to WSS – measure II.3.1

This category of subsidies is very difficult to quantify, but can occur if accounts for different municipal services are not clearly separated. In France, where the private sector is involved in 85% of water, separation of accounts is warranted. Romania and Armenia have created separate legal entities for respective municipal services, and such cross-subsidies cannot occur. Also in Ukraine, urban water supply is mostly separated from the provision of other municipal services.

Therefore, none of the reference countries significantly use cross-subsidies from other municipal services to WSS as a social measure i.e. as a way to keep WSS tariffs below cost recovery. In Moldova, this form of cross subsidy plays only a very minor role and only in some smaller municipalities.

Cross-subsidies from business and institutions to households – measure II.3.2

Table 5.7. **Ratio of industrial to residential tariff rates (the level of cross subsidy)**

	2005	2006	2007	2008	2009	2010	2011	2012
Moldova						3.44	3.53	3.43
Armenia				1.39	1.45	1.39		
Romania				1.37	1.40	1.51		
Ukraine	5.30	4.93	3.25					

Source: IBNET (2014), *The IBNET Water Supply and Sanitation Blue Book 2014.*

The second category of cross-subsidies, which is very common in most countries in South-East Europe (SEE) and Eastern Europe, Caucasus and Central Asia (EECCA), is also used to suppress household tariffs. In France, the law forbids this kind of cross subsidy because similar services must be priced similarly, regardless of the customer. The economic regulator in Moldova has taken the same approach, although cross-subsidies have been the main form of the social support system.

Ukraine allows these cross-subsidies and applies them heavily, as Table 5.7 shows. In Romania, tariffs are supposed to be harmonised, but there are still differences in practice. This is true for many EU accession countries. In Armenia, the legal status of cross-subsidies has not been clarified, but the table shows it happens in practice.

Through tariff differentiation and cross-subsidies, utilities can keep household tariffs significantly below what they would otherwise have to be. If industry pays three times more and consumes only 10% of water sold, the impact on tariffs for residents is already above 20%.

In all reference countries with the exception of France, cross-subsidies from industry to households are perhaps the most significant tool to suppress household tariffs. This is likely to change over time as the result of legislation, better enforcement and independent economic regulation of tariffs. This change will put upward pressure on household tariffs and increase the need to develop other, more cost-effective, pro-poor social support measures.

Cross-subsidies among types of households – measure II.3.3

Cross-subsidies between households are forbidden in France. They have not been found in Armenia and Romania. Ukraine does provide reductions on the bill to certain customers as a form of cross subsidy (see II.4).

Tariff structure or level – measure II.4

Governments often carry out social measures by influencing the tariff structure or level for some or all customers. These measures may be funded either by the government, the operator or a combination of both.

Tariff structure – measure II.4.1

WSS tariff structures influence the distribution of wealth. If they redistribute wealth from richer to poorer customers, they are called progressive. Tariff structures are called regressive if they result in poorer households spending even more of their income on WSS than richer households. The distributional effects of fixed, single volumetric or block tariffs are stronger in EECCA than in Western Europe: in lower- and middle-income countries, households already spend up to five times more of their income on WSS than households in Western Europe do. The distributional effects of tariff structures are proportionally stronger.

For instance, France, Germany and Spain apply a two-part (fixed plus volumetric) tariff structure. However, in France the fixed element in the tariff is small compared to other Western European countries: in Germany, both the annual average water bill and its fixed component are significantly larger, while in Spain, where the annual average WSS bill is at the level of France, the fixed component exceeds 60% of the bill (for more detail see European Environmental Agency [2013]).

In comparison, most Eastern European countries do without any fixed tariff component. On the one hand, this is particularly beneficial for poorer customers. On the other, the single volumetric tariff structure is not conducive towards expanding the network. The variable part of the tariff may be too small to create a business case for expansion. On balance, since increasing coverage is typically funded from outside, the beneficial effect of single volumetric tariffs for poorer customers prevails, compared to a fixed plus single volumetric structure.

Apart from France, all the other **reference countries** use mostly single volumetric tariffs due to a combination of regulation, custom and provisions in loan agreements and other binding documents. In Romania, for instance, single volumetric tariffs are the only ones used. Legally, it is possible to use other tariff structures, but single volumetric tariffs are strongly spelled out by loan agreements and by delegation contracts that local authorities have signed to facilitate regional operations.

Box 5.2. Social aspects of tariff structures

Countries in Southern Europe, Latin America and South East Asia use tariff structures as their primary social support measure in WSS. In particular, these countries use Increasing Block Tariffs (IBTs). Countries in Western Europe have mainly used income support measures.

Germany, as well as England and Wales, apply regressive, fixed plus single volumetric tariff structures. These countries also have a stronger need to apply income support measures.

France does not allow social tariffs i.e. tariffs must be equal for everyone in the service area. But the fixed component in the tariff in France is minimal and IBTs are allowed and occasionally applied. Throughout SEE and EECCA countries, the use of single volumetric tariffs is the dominant form, and IBTs are exceptional.

Income support measures in relation to WSS are rare in these countries; they exist mostly in the form of housing subsidies in large parts of the EECCA region, notably the Russian Federation and Ukraine. The single volumetric tariff structure without WSS-related income assistance is the most common practice. On the one hand, it appears to avoid the social engineering challenge of IBTs by setting brackets and tariffs in a "just and social" way. On the other, it does not require the income assistance that Western European countries must apply to repair the regressive effect of large fixed tariff components.

Source: Verbeeck and Vucijak (2014), *Towards effective social measures in WSS.*

The single volumetric tariff is more progressive than a combination of fixed plus single volumetric. Increasing Block Tariffs (IBTs) are not present in any of the reference countries. Ukraine actively considered IBTs in 2011 and 2012, but has not been able to decide on them.

Despite criticism, many (still) consider IBTs as a good instrument for ensuring affordability of tariffs for the poor. Because of their prevalence in many Southern European countries, Latin America, China and South East Asia, they are discussed separately below in Box 5.2.

In summary, no reference country applies tariff structures as a social measure. Moldova applies a single volumetric tariff, except for two municipalities that apply block tariffs. Therefore, the tariff structure is not widely applied as a social support system in Moldova either.

Tariff choice – measure II.4.2

It can be beneficial for low-income households to switch from unmetered to metered billing of consumption. The idea is that those who would benefit most and those who would need it most are most likely to apply for such a change. In this way, tariff choice can have distinct social benefits.

Metering of water consumption for individual connections has become standard in France much later than the other reference countries. Metering in older apartment blocks remains difficult. In practice, tariff choice is not widely applied as a social measure in any of the reference countries or in Moldova; providing this choice is technically difficult and sometimes costly (e.g. in Moldova, many rural people collect water from stand pipes).

Exemption, ex ante rebates and discounts – measure II.4.3

Because of the large fixed component tariff structures in Western Europe and their regressive effect on income distribution, social measures concentrate on the fixed tariff component. In this way, marginal pricing and scarcity signals are left intact. An example is the exemption from sanitation costs, which is funded through the tax system in the Netherlands. In Flanders, social tariffs are applied in the form of lower IBTs for social cases. In many American cities and Australian states, eligible social cases can obtain various forms of discounts and rebates. These measures are considered tariff-related since they arrive before, or at the moment of, payment of the utility bill (i.e. *ex ante*).

In France, there are no social measures in place that directly reduce the amount of money spent on the water bill. Neither have they been found in any of the other reference countries with the exception of Ukraine. Numerous categories of social groups amounting to over 22% of the population receive privileges in Ukraine. The privilege is provided in the form of a discount of 25%, 50%, 75% or 100% on the consumption norms for various municipal services, including WSS. The social categories also include war veterans and victims of the Chernobyl disaster. These privileges are granted on the basis of national legislation. Moldova does not exempt or provide citizens with discounts in this way.

5.2.3. Income support measures

France provides general income support through the social security system, but not specifically related to WSS expenses. Only some income support measures are allowed in France, namely for those people living in hardship conditions. Similarly, Armenia's social security system only provides general income support not related to specific WSS expenses. Romania does not provide WSS-related income support, either. Ukraine, however, makes abundant use of WSS and other utility services-related income support measures funded by the national government.

Although not widely used in the reference countries, several forms of income assistance can be applied, either to reimburse for payments already made or as a means of payment. These somewhat resemble the exemptions and discounts discussed earlier. It is also possible to reserve support just for those facing hardship. Finally, income support can focus on persons who have already gone into arrears and are working towards a way out. In practice, the various applications are overlapping the categories mentioned below.

Ex post rebates – measure III.1

If a person receives partial reimbursement rather than a discount on the bill itself, the support is considered a form of income support rather than a tariff-related social support. This is because the payment of the bill precedes the benefit. With this form of support, the effect on demand will be small, avoiding the risk of overconsumption of the subsidised

Box 5.3. **Housing subsidies in Ukraine**

Ukraine provides an outstanding example of tied income assistance. Since 1995, the government has provided housing subsidies, which limit expenses for housing and utility services including those for WSS below a certain threshold. These maxima are expressed as a percentage of gross monthly average income and based on the costs incurred on the basis of consumption norms.

Box 5.3. **Housing subsidies in Ukraine** *(continued)*

The percentages are:

- 10% for some households, such as families with children living below subsistence income
- 15% for the remaining households.

Average monthly household income in 2011 was EUR 330, suggesting maximum housing costs of EUR 33 and EUR 50 for the two categories respectively. That means that the part of the housing costs that exceed that amount would be eligible for a subsidy. The subsidies are provided on the condition that WSS bills have been paid. That means eligibility is limited to those with no outstanding debts to utilities or an agreement to repay debt. In 2012, 8% of households in Ukraine received housing subsidies. Although there have been simplifications, the burden limit programme remains complex and costly to administer. Those that qualify have less incentive to limit consumption. The subsidy comes in addition to the privileges, restrictions on cost recovery, cross-subsidies and operating subsidies. Despite costly administration, the system is not well-targeted. Setting the threshold at too low a percentage would include households that are not poor. Setting the threshold too high would mean that income support would only partly reach the poor, while the lion's share would be wasted on subsidies to well-off households. Rural households hardly benefit from housing subsidies.

Source: Komives et al. (2005), *Water, Electricity, and the Poor: Who Benefits from Utility Subsidies?*, and Ukrainian Pilot Project Team of the UNECE (2013), *Assessing progress in achieving equitable access to water and sanitation, pilot project in Ukraine, Country Report.*

good. There will simply be more cash in hand than otherwise. Some of these benefits, however, arrive only well after a person has become a social case and often stay well until after the income situation has improved (OECD, 2002). No widespread applications have been found in any of the reference countries or in Moldova, but examples can again be found in Australia and the United States.

Tied income assistance and vouchers – measure III.2

Ukraine is the only reference country that provides income assistance tied to expenses for WSS and other utility services on a large scale as described in Box 5.3.

France does not provide income assistance directly related to WSS to support regular payment of bills. In Armenia and Romania, income support exists, but is not tied to WSS expenditure at all. In Armenia, the main type of social support is the family benefit system, but this support is not related to actual WSS expenses. Utility bills are used, but only as one of the proxy tests for poverty. The size of one's utility bill is inversely correlated to the

Box 5.4. **The family benefit system in Armenia**

In the late 1990s, Armenia integrated various social support programmes into a single system to provide income support to the poor. The family benefit system provides support roughly to the lowest income quintile of the population. It is a simple non-contributory social safety net that provides financial support, giving priority to the elderly, those with disabilities and poor families

Box 5.4. **The family benefit system in Armenia** *(continued)*

with children. It is a means testing system using such indicators as income, possessions, place of residence and type of residence as proxies. Utilities expenditures actually play a limiting factor in the provision of benefits as they are used as an indicator of wealth. High utility bills suggest more wealth. Beneficiaries also qualify for a free healthcare package. Because of its focus, and its lean and simple set up, the programme is outstanding in the region in terms of efficiency and outreach. The efficiency of the family benefit system contrasts to that of the operating and capital expenditure subsidies in the water sector. The benefits of these subsidies are spread among the entire population and lack the focus on the poor that characterises the family benefit system. Hence, it has been suggested to expand the family benefit system and at the same time reduce operational subsidies to water utilities and allow tariffs to better reflect the financial and economic costs of water supply.

Source: Poghosyan (2014), *Measuring benefit incidence for water subsidization program in Armenia.*

likelihood that someone needs social support. Tied income assistance with respect to WSS expenses has not been found in **Moldova**. Some municipalities, however, do provide such assistance with respect to heating expenses.

France has several important differences from **Romania** and **Armenia:**

- The general social assistance system is much more developed and generous so there is less need for specific WSS-related support.
- Water supply remains a relatively small expense even for poorer households. In the lowest income quintile, it remains below 2% for the lowest income quintile (OECD, 2002, 39).

Other hardship initiatives – measure III.3

In France, there are severe restrictions against operators disconnecting households. For instance, it is forbidden to disconnect a customer if there is a baby or elderly person living in the house or apartment, regardless of the income situation of the household. Furthermore, charitable foundations such as the Salvation Army provide financial and other support in cases of hardship. These kinds of private initiatives also exist in England and Wales, even though disconnections have been outlawed altogether. Such initiatives may also exist in the other reference countries and in Moldova, but could not be identified during this study.

Payment assistance, loans and arrear forgiveness – measure III.4

In France, apart from charities, the operators themselves play an important role in supporting customers that have run into arrears. This makes commercial sense too because of the administrative and legal costs, as well as the negative publicity, that disconnection may generate. Most customers do not willingly enter into arrears and early action on the side of the operator can avoid things getting worse.

Operators, municipalities (owners) and the national government have signed a charter. Funds have been created to provide financial support for applicants in financial hardship. The fund is co-financed by both the national government and through a levy on water

Box 5.5. Social support measure and size of the service area

National or local government may impose social measures, funding them through a variety of channels. Voucher and rebate systems may well be developed for small rural water supply systems. For other social measures, such as (partial) exemption from bills, eligibility is set at a national level; operators have to comply and sometimes fund the measures, regardless of their size or structure. National or local government mostly develop income support measures because of the administration of personal detail regarding household and income. Social support measures for providing access may be carried out locally or by the operator, almost regardless of the size of the service area. The determining factor is the level of solidarity within the community. Social support measures through the tariff level and structure require a minimum level of administration. Still, operators that serve populations of 10 000 or more should normally be able to do so.

Source: Based on authors' findings.

charges collected by the operators. Rather than paying the beneficiaries, it allows for the write-off of arrears on the operators' books. Such mechanisms could not be found in any of the other reference countries or in Moldova.

On the other hand, average spending for WSS in Moldova of 3% of GNI shows that certain parts of the population must spend a vastly higher amount on their water bill (6% or more).

5.3. Conclusion

WSS-related social support measures are vastly different in each of the reference countries. The social measures infrastructure develops in response both to needs and means. Each of the reference countries provides for an approach towards addressing social issues in water supply. This is why the international comparison is of such relevance for Moldova.

In Armenia, social measures in relation to WSS consist mainly of operating and capital expenditure subsidies to operators. At the same time, Armenia runs a comparatively efficient proxy means-testing family benefit system. Given the efficiency of the family-benefit system and the inefficiency of funding tariffs below cost recovery, it has been suggested to expand the system, together with an increase in water tariffs and a reduction in subsidies. The expanded family benefit system may provide more cash income to those who really need it so they can pay for the higher water bill. But this is not the only option. The tariff increase does not have to be universal for all households. The family benefit system may provide benefits in a non-monetary way or in kind, similar to the health care package that is provided. This benefit can take the form of a reduced water bill through social tariffs, a lifeline tariff, vouchers or discounts. It is a clear opportunity to improve targeting of WSS-related social measures in Armenia.

In France, users mostly pay for social measures in the form of solidarity taxes on the water bill. These support investment in rural areas that would otherwise be too expensive. Other WSS-related social measures are limited to non-permanent support in cases of hardship. For this purpose, the general taxpayer also contributes.

In Romania, the focus of social measures has also been on investment in rural areas and increasing connection rates. Whereas this has been a considerable success, there is little or no consideration for affordability constraints of lower income groups. On balance, the lack of access to drinking water is considered a more pressing social issue than the percentage of income spent on the water bill by lower income households. The average Romanian household in 2012 spent 2.7% of income on WSS, suggesting perhaps twice that amount for lower income households.

In contrast, Ukraine does not invest clearly in increasing access to drinking water, but spends heavily on subsidising consumption through a combination of cross-subsidies, operating subsidies, privileges and through the housing subsidy system. The system is not only costly to administer, but also hard to evaluate as people benefit from a combination of below-cost recovery tariffs, discounts and reimbursement.

In all reference countries except Romania, the amount spent on water and sanitation by the population as a whole is at or below 2% of gross national income (GNI). In France, it is even below 1% of average income (OECD, 2002). Making water more affordable to specific social groups would therefore be easier in France. Yet social measures in France are only available for those who are in real hardship.

The need to strengthen social support measures targeted at the poorest part of the population in Moldova is underlined, even though it will be harder to afford it from domestic sources. Household tariffs cannot remain suppressed forever: cross-subsidies must be phased out due to regulatory pressure, or from compliance with loan covenants and because improvements in cost accounting are underway. This further underlines the need and urgency of implementing WSS-related targeted social support measures in Moldova.

The experience of reference countries in this chapter is applied in the scenarios in the next chapter.

References

Barraqué, Bernard and Cédric Le Bris (2007), *Water Sector Regulation in France*, CESifo DICE Report 5 (2), 2007, 4-12, https://www.cesifo-group.de/ifoHome/publications/docbase/details.html?docId=14567363.

European Environment Agency (2013), *Assessment of Cost Recovery Through Water Pricing*, EEA *Technical Report,* No. 16/2013, Copenhagen.

European Union (2009), *European Cohesion Policy in Romania*, Brussels, http://ec.europa.eu/regional_policy/sources/docgener/informat/country2009/ro_en.pdf.

IBNET (2014), *The IBNET Water Supply and Sanitation Blue Book 2014*, The International, Benchmarking Network for Water and Sanitation Utilities Databook/World Bank, Washington, DC.

Komives, K. et al. (2005), *Water, Electricity, and the Poor: Who Benefits from Utility Subsidies?,* World Bank, Washington, DC.

Mascarau, G. (2008), *Le service public d'assainissement non collectif,* quoting BIPE-FP2E 2004.

OECD (2010), *Pricing Water Resources and Sanitation Services*, OECD Publishing, Paris.

OECD (2002), *Social Issues in the Provision and Pricing of Water Services*, OECD Publishing, Paris.

OECD EAP Task Force (2007), *Implementation of a national finance strategy for the water supply and sanitation sector in Armenia, advising the Armenian water authorities on the design and monitoring of a sound tariff policy (Task 3)*, OECD Publishing, Paris.

Poghosyan, S. (2014), *Measuring benefit incidence for water subsidization program in Armenia*, presentation at the methodological conference on measuring social inequality in the South Caucasus and its neighbourhood, Yerevan, 2014.

Ukrainian Pilot Project Team of the UNECE (2013), *Assessing progress in achieving equitable access to water and sanitation, pilot project in Ukraine, Country Report*, United Nations Economic Commission for Europe, www.unece.org/fileadmin/DAM/env/water/activities/Equitable_access/Country_report__Pilot_project_Ukraine_rev.pdf.

Verbeeck, G. and B. Vucijak (2014), *Towards effective social measures in WSS*, presentation at the conference on regional water utility management, Tirana, 5-7 November 2014, http://balkansjointconference.org/wp-content/uploads/2014/11/Giel-Verbeeck-Towards-effective-social-measures-in-WSS..pdf.

WB & IAWD, (2009), *Danube Water Program*, World Bank, Washington, DC; International Association of Water Supply Companies in the Danube River Catchment Area, Vienna, World Bank and Inter-American Development Bank, www.danube-water-program.org/media/DWP_brochure-MAIL_0914.pdf.

Zetland, D. (2014), *Living with Water Scarcity*, Aquanomics Press, Amsterdam.

Chapter 6

Enhancement of domestic financial support mechanisms for water supply and sanitation in Moldova: Scenario analysis

This chapter outlines four imaginary yet realistic scenarios with respect to both supply-side and demand-side support measures. Further, it presents ex ante analysis and prioritisation of the scenarios to inform the choice to be made by local decision makers.

The previous chapter has considered the experience from four reference countries in the application of social support measures in water supply. Social policies typically focus on the demand side. Supply side measures may not be part of a social policy, but do generate vast social benefits, particularly if there is not yet universal access to water supply and sanitation (WSS). A summary of findings from reference countries indicate that those countries apply various models, but some useful cases can be extracted from each of them.

In Armenia, financing mechanisms that address social aspects in relation to WSS are provided mainly to the supply side in the form of operating and capital expenditure subsidies to operators. At the same time, Armenia runs a comparatively efficient proxy means-tested family benefit system that helps support the demand side (not only WSS-related). Given the efficiency of the family benefit system and the inefficiency of using tariffs below cost recovery, it has been suggested to expand the family benefit system, together with an increase in water tariffs and phasing out blind subsidies. The expanded family benefit system may provide more cash income to those who really need it, so that they can pay for a higher water bill. The country's political economy and current economic challenges impact the pace of the introduction of more demand-side financial support mechanisms in the WSS sector.

In France, users pay for social measures in the form of solidarity taxes on the water bill. These support investment in developing WSS in rural areas that would otherwise be much slower. Other WSS-related social measures are limited to non-permanent support in cases of hardship. For this purpose, the general taxpayer also contributes.

In Romania, social measures have also focused on investment in rural WSS and increasing connection rates. Whereas this has been a considerable success, there is little or no consideration for affordability constraints of lower income groups. On balance, the lack of access to drinking water is considered a more pressing social issue than the percentage of income spent on the water bill for lower income households. Some may say that Romania's WSS-related social policy is supply-side oriented. Others may say, however, there is no WSS-related social policy at all.

Ukraine does not invest clearly in increasing access to drinking water, but spends heavily on subsidising consumption through a combination of cross-subsidies, operating subsidies, privileges and through the housing subsidy system. The system is not only costly to administer, but also hard to evaluate as people benefit from a combination of below cost recovery tariffs, discounts and reimbursements.

The often applied, but ultimately unsuccessful approach, would involve opting for the most appealing country and agreeing on the intent to copy the associated measures. This, however, would not do justice to the complexity of the Moldovan situation. There is no point in opting for country X or country Y per se. Institutional structures are different in Armenia from Moldova; France's per capita income is 8.5 times higher; Romania is an EU member.

However, the consideration of its own and other countries' experiences does help Moldova in formulating its own specific strategy. The proposed way forward here is to:

- Agree on the current situation.
- Distinguish between temporary fixes and structural solutions.
- Formulate realistic scenarios reflecting possible real developments.
- Agree on which scenario would be optimal.
- Define policy actions, including risk mitigation measures.

The first two steps may have been taken already as part of the National Policy Dialogue. If there is consensus on the analysis of the previous chapters, one can proceed on the subsequent steps, starting with the formulation of scenarios.

This study has developed **four imaginary yet realistic scenarios** with respect to both supply-side and demand-side measures; they focus on social measures supporting the demand for WSS services as the latter are especially weak in Moldova. The scenarios feature simultaneous measures on both supply and demand sides where possible; the overall public finance management (PFM) system in the WSS sector will benefit if both demand- and supply-side measures are pursued and complement each other. After outlining these scenarios, the study makes an *ex ante* evaluation on the basis of the following criteria:

- institutional aspects, policy implementation feasibility and uncertainty
- social outcome
- economic and environmental outcome.

6.1. Scenario A: No policy intervention

6.1.1. Policy package

There are simply no further initiatives to either strengthen existing policies or develop new ones. The existing situation, described in Chapter 4, is characterised by:

- unclear legal mandate of the regulator
- no social policy responsibility for the regulatory system, the economic regulator and regulation
- no changes in allocation of funds for investment
- no follow up on regionalisation initiatives.

There is no follow up on recommendations with respect to better co-ordination of the National Environmental Fund (NEF) and the National Fund for Regional Development (NRFD), use of the same time horizon for planning, use of the same sets of performance indicators on WSS and use of a performance-based financing model.

6.1.2. Result

There is no adjustment or further development of existing policies under this scenario. Municipalities and Apacanals continue with "business as usual". Attempts to regionalise operations fail because of various reasons (opposition, lack of organisation, lack of funds, legal and bureaucratic/institutional obstacles).

Existing social measures remain intact. The regulator cannot enforce the phase out of cross subsidisation from businesses to households. The authority of the National Agency for Regulation in Energy (ANRE) is challenged. It is unclear who is responsible for tariff setting (municipalities or ANRE). As a consequence, tariff increases are not carried out at all.

Apacanals struggle to make ends meet, but are unable to adjust staffing to more economic levels. Financial statements present gradually increasing losses of the WSS system and financial sustainability of operators is endangered. A few larger Apacanals try to develop a social policy on their own initiative. Because of lack of central guidance, these initiatives fail to take off or to obtain municipal or regulatory approval. The only measure that succeeds in one town is a free amount of 5 m^3 (a so-called first block) for every customer (billing point). Because there is no associated tariff increase, this squeezes the revenues at the expense of funds for maintenance for the Apacanal concerned.

Because there are no alternative social measures, the political acceptability of tariff increases remains severely restricted. External finance for Apacanals is severely limited because tariff increases are a *de facto* condition for external finance (either domestic or foreign). The required investment in infrastructure cannot be financed. As a consequence, potential willingness to pay (for better service) cannot be realised.

Lack of investment in municipal infrastructure holds back economic growth. Poverty increases, thus also reducing the ability to pay.

Growth in access to water and sanitation stagnates. Prospects for a better life diminish for the poorer parts of the population and there is growing dissatisfaction. Because of poor water quality, people spend a substantial and growing part of their income on bottled water. Urbanisation continues unabatedly. The security of water supply is increasingly at risk.

A vicious circle of deterioration is evident to everyone, but none of the stakeholders can act for fear of political unrest, job security or tariff increases.

This scenario undermines the economic foundation of WSS by utilities. Sooner or later, local government will have to take over provision of services or they will collapse. Utilities services will become government services as there will be no business case for delegated provision. Funding for the sector will depend wholly on the fiscal budget. This scenario is unacceptable to any responsible policy maker.

6.2. Scenario B: All cards on water supply

6.2.1. Policy package

The second scenario does nothing beyond existing measures on social policies. However, it addresses social aspects through increased investment (particularly in accessibility of WSS services) and through regionalisation, resulting in urban areas *de facto* cross subsidising rural areas.

First, this involves follow up on recommendations with respect to better co-ordination of the NEF and NRFD, use of the same time horizon for planning, use of the same sets of performance indicators on WSS and use of a performance-based financing model.

Domestic financial resources are spent to maximise total investment in the sector either financed from loans or grants. Affordability is considered a secondary priority because accessibility comes first.

The number of operators in Moldova is reduced from over 1 000 to a few dozen. Regional operators receive temporary regulatory waivers when it comes to quality and safety standards in some of their service areas of responsibility. Although tariffs do go up everywhere, a cross subsidy from urban to rural areas remains in place; this is because tariffs are harmonised over the enlarged service area, whereas the costs of service to more rural areas is higher. The government actively monitors and publishes connection rates for water supply and sanitation services. Otherwise, both the central and local government ignore social issues.

6.2.2. Result

There is rapid expansion in external finance. International financial institutions (IFIs) are interested in working with expanded regional operators. As a result, access to drinking water and sanitation is expanded and/or service level increases. Government monitors connection rates more thoroughly as they are explicit policy objectives with explicit target indicators.

Over four years, tariffs rise drastically, partly due to debt covenant stipulations and partly as a result of new economic regulation. Because there is no differentiated tariff for the poor, tariff increases become increasingly controversial.

Regional operators get off to a difficult start. Urban customers feel that time and attention go to the periphery. Customers in the periphery face higher tariffs and see no tangible improvements. The regional company does not have a local office. The regional operators have not yet developed customer service that improves on the local operator. Staff optimisations (downsizing) lead to controversy and attempts to damage the reputation of the regional management. After about four-five years, however, the perception of regional operators improves, as people learn about similar approaches in countries with advanced regionalisation (Romania and Kosovo). By that time, benefits of the investments become clear to the customer. Water resources improve because of massive investment also in wastewater treatment.

6.3. Scenario C: Framework for decentralised WSS social measures

6.3.1. Policy package

Most stakeholders agree that social measures are important. It is also believed that customisation is essential and no one size fits all. When it comes to social measures, local communities know best how to achieve affordability and whom to support. Local communities need tools and means, but can opt for their own individual social support scheme. This may be a combination of a variety of supply, tariff-related and income-related measures, depending on whether the community is a small village, a mid-size town or big city.

Others are less optimistic, but acknowledge that central government has neither the capacity nor the political will nor the legal mandate to implement WSS social measures across the country. It therefore opts for an approach that involves all stakeholders through dialogue and exchange.

All Apacanals and all municipalities – be they small or big ones – are invited to take part in such exchanges on social measures. Because there is no enforcement, the government encourages exploring all possible measures. A toolkit is distributed that describes all the measures together with their advantages and drawbacks. Social measures in WSS vary from municipality to municipality. In the capital and some larger cities, there are some successful attempts at developing social measures. These are based on voluntary co-operation between the municipality and the Apacanal.

There are discussions with ANRE on whether any alternative tariff structure than the single volumetric tariff structure is allowed. Some municipalities are interested in establishing a two-part (dual rate) tariff structure. Others want to apply IBT, providing a water allowance for the first 5 m^3 to all or else a selection of household customers. Yet other municipalities consider vouchers, support in debt rescheduling, temporary hardship relief and subsidies for water-saving measures. The latter type of initiatives even receive donor assistance.

Municipalities are free to adopt their own affordability criteria and develop policies to keep tariffs affordable for lower income groups.

As a variation in this scenario, there is a follow-up recommendation on supply side measures made in Chapter 7 of this report with respect to better co-ordination of the NEF and NRFD. It recommends using the same time horizon for planning and the same sets of performance indicators on WSS, as well as a performance-based financing model.

6.3.2. Result

There is a lot of debate about social measures in WSS. Policies are developed in bigger cities; most smaller municipalities opt to wait for results in these cities. None of the municipalities or Apacanals has budgeted for social measures. There are therefore no funds for implementation and most initiatives fail for that reason.

For a number of Apacanals and municipalities, the only affordable social measures are cross-subsidies from businesses and industries to households. Without support from central government, they would not implement any additional measures. Other municipalities consider that social cases need to pay for utility bills from general income support that they may or may not receive.

The flow of external finance stagnates because there is no further push to regionalisation. As long as discussions about tariffs and affordability continue, the revenue generating capacity of Apacanals is unclear. Access to water and sanitation stagnates.

Social measures are developed in a few bigger cities, but overall the situation remains much the same for everyone. If there is a follow up on the supply side measures, the picture is slightly more positive because use of government funds becomes more efficient. However, these gains are small compared to social losses from stagnated external financing associated with this scenario.

6.4. Scenario D: Centralised WSS social measures

6.4.1. Policy package

The government agrees on a national pro-poor programme targeting the 20% lowest income quintile of the Moldovan population. It aims at ensuring the target group has access to drinking water and sanitation at an affordable price.

The programme involves a number of radical and ambitious policy interventions. With respect to the water sector, focus has shifted from universally low household tariffs towards universal access to service. Covenants with Apacanals agree on investment support in exchange for increasing service areas, increasing access and for achieving milestones in regionalisation of operations.

The government uses a uniform affordability threshold for WSS tariffs. Tariffs are considered too high for the population at large if WSS costs exceed 5% of average household income; to that end, utilities subject to independent economic regulation must fulfil additional reporting requirements.

The independent regulator monitors, and reports annually on, access and affordability of services for lower income groups. The regulatory system undertakes policy response measures (e.g. revising investment plans on the supply side, or increasing targeted social support measures to vulnerable households on the demand side) to address the affordability problem if, when and where it arises.

The water tariff moves quickly towards full cost recovery through a combination of measures. First, ANRE applies stringent efficiency criteria for staff per 1 000 population, although that is corrected for the level of urbanisation of a service area. This limits the potential tariff increase. Second, ANRE recognises maintenance needs and costs of asset renewal, which increase the cost recovering tariff. Third, ANRE and external financiers insist on transparency and public access to information. Most regional operators create a Maintenance Replacement and Development Fund, following the example of Romania. As a result, funds earmarked for investment are managed transparently and cannot be used for other purposes. Also the proportion of funds spent on improving access to WSS services can be extracted transparently. Finally, the government promotes public scrutiny by requiring transparent publicly accessible reporting formats.

On balance household tariffs move upward drastically, also because of the harmonisation of the tariff across customer groups.

A water abstraction and water pollution fee is implemented, and Apacanals also pay. These provide funding for the investment committed as part of the covenants. Polluting industries, however, contribute proportionally more. These charges provide incentives that lead to the protection of water resources. These can be seen as a social measure for future generations. But the charges also further increase the total household water bill and the need to support the lowest income quintile with targeted measures.

Regional water utilities can take part in a social scheme aimed at poor households. Registered, means-tested poor households are eligible for water-related social measures. There is a range of such measures available. The most important ones are the following:

- Access support

  Registered social cases may file for a subsidy equivalent to the cost of providing access to water and sanitation. The aim is to lift people out of poverty by improving access to drinking water and sanitation. Funding for the scheme is split evenly between the government and the regional operator. It is expected the regional operator will earn back the connection costs over the subsequent years.

- Consumption rebate

  Registered social cases are eligible to a lump sum discount on the water bill equivalent to the lower value of:

  - the water bill
  - the equivalent cost of a monthly amount of 5 m^3 per household, or, if it can be administered, 1 m^3 per person in that household.

The sum of the discounts provided is transferred directly from the social security service to the regional operator. Households are eligible for this scheme if they are registered social cases and if not in default on their (rescheduled) payments to the regional operators. Annex 5 elaborates this idea/proposal in more detail.

Similarly to the earlier case, a variation to this scenario is a follow up recommendation on the supply side measures with respect to better co-ordination of the NEF and NRFD in regards to use of the same time horizon for planning, use of the same sets of performance indicators on WSS and use of a performance-based financing model.

6.4.2. Result

Household surveys show that access to safe drinking water and sanitation improves. Because there is a much smaller financial constraint, the willingness to be connected to safe drinking water sources increases. Overall, tariffs increase and household tariffs rise even higher. However, for the poorest part of the population, the share of household (HH) income spent on piped or bottled water stabilises. Water consumption per capita continues to decline, putting upward pressure on tariffs. This project does not have reliable data on actual price elasticity of water demand in Moldova. However, international experience suggests the elasticity is in the range from -0.3 to -0.6 (see Nauges and Wittington [2010]). All things being equal, as the price for water increases, per capita consumptions lowers. Therefore, some noticeable decrease of the per capita consumption is expected in Moldova, too.

External finance grows, mostly in the form of supra national loan financing by international financial institutions. Apacanals commercialise rapidly as a result of the financial straightjacket. This is created by a combination of debt service obligations, strict economic regulation and the duty to account transparently for various costs, particularly those for maintenance and investment. Improvements in asset management will likely reduce total long-term costs (O&M plus investment).

If there is also follow up on supply side measures, the picture is even better, because of the enhanced efficiency in the use of government funds. However, these gains are relatively small compared to the social gains associated with improved external financing under this scenario.

6.5. Evaluation and conclusion

Although these scenarios can outline possible development, the study has made a brief *ex ante* evaluation based on 1) institutional aspects, policy implementation feasibility and uncertainty; 2) social outcome; and 3) economic and environmental outcome.

Institutional aspects, policy implementation feasibility and uncertainty

Almost by definition, the first scenario is the easiest one to implement, especially in the political economy context of Moldova. The result can also be predicted with more certainty than the other scenarios, i.e. financial unsustainability of the system will consume more and more resources from the state and, eventually, from households without significant achievements and progress of the WSS system and social aspects of water supply.

The second scenario has a relatively predictable outcome, but institutional challenges make it difficult to realise. It involves a *de facto*, if not *de jure,* transfer of power from the municipalities to the centre. This causes another type of uncertainty.

The third scenario involves a new policy instrument in the form of voluntary co-operation under the co-ordination of central government. The process will lead to agreements and decentralised policies, but one cannot specify the outcome of the process. Voluntary co-operation also requires a level of sophistication and reliability from the partners involved. Perhaps only a few municipalities will be able to develop viable policies, customised for their circumstances.

The fourth scenario requires co-ordinated financial and social policy, and budget systems with a reliable and trusted targeting system of identification of the target segments of beneficiaries for the financial and social support mechanisms.

Social outcome

As has been argued, the social outcome of the first scenario is not acceptable. There would be no improvement for the poorest part of the population. In the second scenario, there may be improvement, but it would be realised merely through the supply side. Other possible solutions will not be considered. The third scenario provides for ample consideration and discussion. The problems of water supply to lower income groups will be the focus. It is unclear, however, whether there is going to be any practical follow up on these problems. The fourth scenario will provide solutions, but perhaps with comparatively little consideration on whether these are required and practical at the local level. If the policy mix is good and the implementation successful, it could bring substantial benefits to the poor in the entire country.

Economic and environmental outcome

The first scenario would also generate unacceptable results for the economy and environment, simply because there is no improvement and eventual deterioration is foreseen. The second scenario would bring substantial economic and environmental benefits to current and future generations alike. Results of the third scenario depend on local stakeholders, but due to reduced external finance the economic and environmental effects will be disappointing. The fourth scenario has the potential of generating as good or nearly as good economic and environmental results as the second. This is because of the strong central government and implementation of economic instruments. With social measures, an important obstacle to overall tariff increases ceases to be relevant.

The scenarios outlined do not allow for estimated future sector performance ratios. This would simply be too subjective. It is possible, however, based on the above, to indicate performance of each scenario for each evaluation criterion (Table 6.1).

Table 6.1. **Indicative relative performance for each scenario for each evaluation criterion**

	Institutional	Social	Economic/ environmental	Total unweighted
A. No policy intervention	x	x	x	x
B. All cards on water supply	45	35	45	125
C. Framework for decentralised WSS social measures	35	15	15	70
D. Centralised WSS social measures	20	50	40	110
Total	≡100	≡100	≡100	≡300

Note: **x**: not applicable.

Source: Authors' findings.

Table 6.1 is necessarily the result of a subjective valuation as is the weighting of evaluation criteria. In the table, each criterion weighs equally. However, the evaluation does highlight the following:

- There is a need to establish additional social measures in WSS. Carrying on existing measures will lead to an unacceptable social and economic outcome.
- Social measures are complex to carry out. Either one must overcome obstacles to centralised intervention or rely on a decentralised approach that may result in an incoherent flurry of measures and initiatives.

- There is no significant difference in the economic and environmental effects of Scenario B and Scenario D.
- The socio-economic gains associated with Scenario C look disappointing compared to the policy effort required.
- The social gains associated with Scenario D compared to B are significant, but not huge. Is it worth overcoming the policy obstacles in the legal, institutional and organisational field? Is there sufficient political will and agreement to establish such a policy package? In other words, is it not better to focus just on water supply and leave the social questions to resolve themselves through economic growth and local solutions and initiatives?

Policy makers shall make their own evaluation. This study has primarily sought to provide a framework for discussion and to illustrate policy choices and trade-offs.

A summary of key findings and conclusions, together with recommendations, is provided in the final chapter.

Reference

Nauges C. and D. Wittington (2010), "Estimation of water demand in developing countries: An Overview", *World Bank Research Observer*, Vol. 25/2, Washington, DC.

Chapter 7

A summary of key findings, conclusions and recommendations

This chapter presents a short summary of key findings and conclusions of the report, as well as key recommendations. It was drafted to serve (and de facto was used) as a stand-alone short policy summary of this study to be circulated and discussed with key local stakeholders in the framework of the National Policy Dialogue on water policy in Moldova.

Water supply is an important responsibility of the Moldovan government. Public finance flows related to water supply and sanitation (WSS), including Apacanals, are also significant. The international community is still a key source of financing investments in the sector and the country uses an incomplete set of financial and social support mechanisms and in uncoordinated way.

There are significant challenges in the WSS sector in Moldova.

- The infrastructure is well beyond its optimal level in two ways:
    - It is deteriorated and significant capital investments are required in the near future to maintain quality of services.
    - Socio-demographic changes in the country in recent decades affecting the density and volume of the demand (i.e. WSS systems are now often oversized compared with the actual population size and the demand for WSS from households in respective communities). This factor has even more impact when using old Soviet standards and norms for construction of new WSS systems; meanwhile, the consumption pattern has significantly changed in recent years, especially after wide application of metering and due to high labour migration.
- Meeting the targets set in the national strategies on environmental and WSS sectors and the EU Association agreement, including the need for significant WSS infrastructure extension (especially in rural areas).
- Fragmentation of accountability, and poor planning and co-ordination systems to drive policy and result-based (programme-based) budgeting in the WSS sector.
- Poor coverage and quality of WSS services, which slows down economic development in rural areas.
- Lack of effective combination of demand- and supply-side financial support mechanisms that will also be linked with the social policies, etc.
- The sector's financial sustainability. Until recently, local public administrations (LPAs) set WSS tariffs hypothetically taking into consideration social aspects. They did not fully cover operation and maintenance (O&M) costs, nor could they provide for investment. The National Agency for Regulation in Energy (ANRE) is now responsible for tariff setting: it declared an objective of full financial and economic cost recovery, but outcomes are yet to be seen. ANRE's shift calls for much stronger and, importantly, well co-ordinated social support mechanisms targeted at vulnerable households and generating high value for money.
- Explicit and implicit subsidy of the WSS sector by the government and municipalities, which diverts scarce resources from investments in the sector to operational support with poor efficiency gains.
- Heavy dependence on donor community in allocating capital investments in the WSS sector.

As indicated in this report, the most important mid-term challenges the WSS faces are the need to:

- Improve sector co-ordination both on planning and delivery sides aimed at improving the deteriorated infrastructure and quality of WSS services.
- Improve efficiency through optimising the size (downsizing) of WSS systems and staff.

- Meet the requirements of the national strategies for environment and water, as well as the EU Water Framework Directive (WFD) and other WSS-related European Commission directives.
- Improve coverage and extend networks, especially in rural areas to achieve the "Water for All" policy objective.

Meeting these challenges will contribute to environment, health and economic growth. The status quo, however, will contribute to sustaining poverty and making the country more vulnerable in the context of climate change.

7.1. Summary of financial support mechanisms

As indicated earlier, households and businesses generate the major portion of financial flows in the WSS sector and the amounts increase on an annual basis (see Table 7.1).

Table 7.1. **Total sales and water fees collected by largest water utilities in Moldova in 2009-13**

in MDL thousands

	2009	2010	2011	2012	2013
Income from water supply sales	463 673.8	573 670.5	572 617.7	605 597.8	612 371.8
Income from water sanitation sales	194 190.8	217 978.7	217 424.4	225 926.6	230 702.4
Total sales of Apacanals	**657 864.6**	**791 649.2**	**790 042.1**	**831 524.4**	**843 074.2**

Source: Based on AMAC (Association of Moldova Apacanals) database, www.amac.md.

The country's development partners also play a significant role in financing of the WSS sector in Moldova, providing funds foremost for capital investments. Table 7.2 presents the loans and grants to the sector that are channelled via the national budget system.

Table 7.2. **WSS sector grants and loans provided by donors and channelled via national budget system**

in MDL thousands

	2009	2010	2011	2012	2013	2014 (plan)
Grants	250 859	159 342	1 485	183 985	69 219	146 236
Loans	16 586.3	73 015.5	44 923.0	106 500.5	182 059.0	62 566.7
Total	**267 445**	**232 358**	**46 408**	**290 486**	**251 278**	**208 803**

Source: Based on MOF data.

Apart from financial support from development partners, the WSS sector in Moldova also receives significant funding from domestic financial sources (central and district/ rayon budgets). The main actors from the state are the Ministry of Environment (MOE) and the Ministry of Regional Development and Construction (MRDC). Both organisations have dedicated funds (National Environmental Fund [NEF] and National Fund for Regional Development [NFRD]) that formulate the major portion of the government's cash contribution to the sector. Overall, the state budget is the second largest financier of the sector after the businesses and households that pay for the WSS services to the Apacanals.

Table 7.3. **Actual state budget allocations for WSS, by subsectors**

in MDL thousands

	2009	2010	2011	2012	2013
Environment protection	132 155.9	155 407.7	190 515.0	238 466.9	326 717.2
Utilities	2 147.2	38 888.8	123 508.0	139 048.2	329 504.9
Total state budget expenditures in WSS	**134 303.2**	**194 296.5**	**314 023.0**	**377 515.1**	**656 222.1**

Source: Based on BOOST database, http://wbi.worldbank.org/boost/boost-initiative.

In 2013, the sector has overall generated around MDL 1.75 billion of financial flows with almost half of it from households. Despite the common perception on absence of subsidies of the WSS sector, direct cash support in various forms (mainly for capital construction activities) is half of the total flows (as per Table 7.4 indicating the shares in 2013). This means the sector is not financially self-sustainable and far from reaching self-sustainability in the mid-term horizon.

Table 7.4. **Summary of WSS financial flows in 2013**

	2013 (in MDL thousands)	Percentage of total
Water users (households payments to Apacanals)	843 074	48
Ministry of Environment	592 304	34
Donors (via national PFM system), including loans	251 278	14
Ministry of Regional Development and Construction	63 918	4
Total	**1 750 574**	**100**

Source: Based on BOOST database, http://wbi.worldbank.org/boost/boost-initiative, MOF data.

Moreover, due to widespread poverty and tough affordability constraints, a switch to full financial self-sustainability of the sector is neither feasible nor recommended for the near future. This study has revealed that continuation of both supply side efforts and introduction of effective demand-side support mechanisms is inevitable and highly desired in the current circumstances.

In addition, citizens of Moldova also support the WSS sector via indirect financial support mechanisms not visible in current public financial management (PFM) systems. In particular, Apacanals receive subsidies, as well as generate significant financial losses. The latter is also a type of expense as the ownership of those Apacanals is public. However, these expenses are not in cash terms. In any case, citizens pay and will continue to pay for these losses whether they notice or not. A non-representative survey by the project revealed around MDL 100 million of annual loss in 12 main Apacanals that provided information on their financial positions.

The government of Moldova supports the sector on the supply side by financing various investment projects aimed at improving the network, increasing the quality of the services and expanding coverage. Persistence of such supply-side support policy is inevitable, as the sector needs it in the mid- to long-term horizon. The critical argument is that general social policies (i.e. state support on the demand side) may make WSS services affordable, but cannot make it accessible, safe and sufficient. Having said that, however, the application of supply-side financial support mechanisms in the sector needs to be improved. Existence of several national and regional, but separate, supply-side mechanisms and initiatives (NEF, NFRD and donors) present significant challenges regarding the coherence of implemented policies between various actors. This challenge could have been partially solved if solid regional planning systems were in place, which would drive all initiatives in a synergetic way. However, budget planning and programme-driven policy decision-making systems must be enhanced in the country both at central and regional levels. The discussion at the National Policy Dialogue meeting in November 2014 confirmed the majority of donors do not channel their investments in the WSS sector via a national PFM system. The government should also invite the donor community to integrate its financial support mechanisms more into the national PFM systems or, at least, perform policies that are more coherent.

Supply-side financial support mechanisms and policies must also rely more on modern infrastructure construction and design standards. They need to mitigate the risks of having initially oversized infrastructure that will boost not only development costs, but also O&M costs. Such inaccuracies and oversights will then transform the financial burden on consumers and, inevitably, on regional or central PFM systems (via explicit or implicit transformation mechanisms).

At the same time, direct social support mechanisms are not adequate to support the demand of those who need such support. The direct WSS-related financial support to vulnerable households does not exist at the central level and is non-systemic and insignificant at local governments and Apacanal levels. Local public authorities try to provide some indirect support via below cost recovery tariff regulations. ANRE is introducing a new methodology based on a purely commercial footing. New challenges appear with the introduction of such models and methodologies (including possible withdrawal of cross-subsidies from businesses to households).

The latter will increase social pressure and require the government to consider alternative means of support mechanisms in the near future. However, in one way or another, social protection measures should be an integral part of the system for economic regulation with more actors involved in the process, including the Ministry of Labour, Social Protection and Family.

The institutional framework of the WSS sector is complex. Various actors from the governance side in the sector, as well as donors sometimes lack integration with national policies and systems. The Moldovan WSS sector governance and regulation is also fragmented. No single body is responsible for the whole sector. Social, tariff, investment and sector policy making is divided among various actors. Sector planning and financial flows are often not synchronised. Affordability of tariffs is different because of a) uneven distribution of income among urban and rural areas and among regions; and b) different tariff levels/rates across settlements.

Integrated programmes must be developed, providing solutions both on:

- the supply side i.e. access to quality WSS
- the demand side i.e. affordability of service.

Financing will have to optimise domestic and external sources, ideally in integrated co-financed programmes. Considering the associated financial challenge, there is a need to focus strongly, if not exclusively, on the poor. The poor are concentrated mostly in rural areas.

The social measures in a broad sense are implemented not in isolation but against a background of major trends:

- Regionalisation of services and optimisation of business models

Romania has been leading the way in showing that it can happen without compromising local legal competences.

- Economic regulation of WSS

Moldova has taken an important step forward by expanding the mandate of ANRE to regulate WSS tariffs. The practical implementation of this expanded mandate is happening, but outcomes are yet to be seen.

- Cost recovery

Funding for investment in WSS increasingly depends on the willingness to charge cost-recovering tariffs and eliminate counter-productive cross-subsidies.

- Economic instruments

Governments need to apply economic instruments for environmental policies, some of which will affect the WSS bill. Environmental charges on water abstraction and pollution are one possibility that will directly or indirectly affect the costs of WSS services.

Both cost recovery and the application of economic instruments are required to eliminate the present over-reliance on external EU-funded support.

- Improved public financial management

Sector fragmentation (including on PFM aspects with various in-budget and off-budget implementation mechanisms with lack of co-ordinated policy-budget linkage) carries a major risk of low effectiveness and performance of investments. This couples with use of old standards that have significant implication on the cost and payment period of investments.

- Improved WSS-sector planning process at national and regional levels

Bottom-up and top-down planning processes must drive investment strategies and decisions. A fragmented system of planning and investment project decision-making processes (including various national and donor organisations actively present in the sector) must work in a more synergetic and integrated form.

The standards for constructing and operating WSS systems must be improved if investment flows are to be expanded, tariffs increased and social support mechanisms developed.

7.2. Existing water-related social support systems in Moldova

Table 7.5 presents a summary of social support measures identified in the water sector that affect accessibility and affordability of WSS services (for more detail see Chapter 4).

None of the social support measures, however, is targeting the poor very specifically:

- Existing capital expenditure subsidies are not targeted, although network extensions typically benefit households with below average income.
- Existing tariff-related measures tend to suppress all household tariffs instead of subsidising only the poor.

- Income-related measures with respect to WSS hardly exist in Moldova.

The assessment in this report suggests that social support measures that are used most heavily in Moldova provide little value for money. The social return on the (cross) subsidies is very low and these are the most common measurers. The three social support systems that perform relatively well are all three much smaller in size.

These are capital expenditure subsidies, indirect support and WSS-related income support.

In sum, water-related domestic social support systems (i.e. demand side support) in Moldova are underdeveloped. For the poorest 20% of the population, very little is available in terms of discount, hardship relief or support to become connected to the system.

As a minimum, the results of the assessment illustrate:

- the need to rethink the provision of water-related social support
- the need for an integrated approach towards the design of alternatives
- the need to put the primary beneficiary of these measures in the centre (i.e. the lowest income quintile).

Table 7.5. **Summary of identified domestic social support systems in Moldova**

	Social support system	Effect	Form
I. Supply-related measures	Capital expenditure subsidy	Lowering capital expenditure costs of respective WSS providers	Grant or in-kind donation from local or national government or domestic charity organisation
II. Tariff-related measures	Operating expenditure subsidy	Reducing the discrepancy between operating income and operating expenditure of respective WSS providers	Grant or in-kind donation from local or national government
	Indirect support	Allowing for continuation of services from WSS provider to vulnerable customer	Formal or informal measures that ease access to, or the costs of, WSS, such as disconnection policies, lifelines, entitlements
	Cross-subsidies	Cross-subsidies help soften affordability constraints faced by subsidised consumer groups, but often force industries to build their own boreholes and surface water intakes, thus undermining the revenue base of Apacanals	Cross-subsidies between municipal services, between WSS customer groups and between WSS household customers
III. Income-related measures	Water-related income support	Improving income situation of WSS clients to pay their bills	National or local social benefits, earmarked for water-related expenses

Source: Authors' findings.

7.3. Lessons from reference countries

The study has considered the experience with social measures for WSS in reference countries (Armenia, France, Romania and Ukraine) presented in the sections above. The overall lessons from the reference countries are as follows:

1. A more or a less centralised form of social measures

In the case of Armenia, one can build on the already existing and well-functioning family benefit system, which is absent in other countries. Government can develop targeted assistance measures with existing regional operators in such an environment.

2. More or less focus on cost recovery

France and Romania focus on cost recovery and, hence, on the sustainability of supply. In the long term, this ensures the widest access to service. However, there is perhaps less attention for supporting social needs of existing customers. While Ukraine, on the other hand, considers customers' ability to pay, the financial conditions for the utilities are dire. This does not help establish conditions for improving supply through external finance i.e. revenue-generating capacity and independent management.

3. Degree of SMART-ness

As Ukraine illustrates, a large number of overlapping measures is generally not benefiting the poorest part of the population. Up to one-third of the population benefits from the system of subsidies, tariff repression and examples; it is completely untraceable how these benefits actually help. In summary, measures should be SMART (Specific, Measureable, Attainable, Relevant and Time-bound). Annex 5 provides an illustration of a SMART social support measure in WSS.

The above findings and analysis frames the nature of recommendations into two main categories:

- Improving planning and budgeting systems to increase efficiency of existing financial mechanisms.
- Moving towards systemic change by enhancing the nature and scope of the domestic financial support mechanisms for two reasons:
  - International practice suggests more comprehensive approaches of balancing supply- and demand-side financial support mechanisms to be employed by countries. The scope and scale of support mechanisms is country-specific, but a combination is recommended based on international experience.
  - The country has already initiated reforms that will drive towards a more effective and sustainable WSS system. However, the current range of reforms does not adequately address the challenges that will inevitably emerge for quite a significant portion of the population. Negligence of such challenges and setbacks may endanger the pace and smoothness of reforms in WSS sector.

7.4. Options for improving the WSS sector planning and budgeting systems

Addressing sector fragmentation

As presented in the sections above, the institutional arrangement for the WSS sector is quite fragmented in Moldova, especially as it relates to WSS investment policy, administration and accountability. The current arrangement carries the risks of both overlapping and omitting the real sector policy and financing needs. Duplication of mandates and coverage of intervention mechanisms is particularly apparent in the cases of MOE and MRDC.

Sector co-ordination does not necessarily change budget implementation arrangements and/or institutional aspects of project administration. Instead, co-ordination requires organisation of information flows in a way that policy decisions and accountability match budget decisions and accountability. If this fails, then the budgeting system will not be integrated into the WSS sector policy and monitoring and evaluation (M&E) systems. In any case, streamlining the lines of WSS sector planning, budgeting and accountability will not necessarily lead to re-arrangements in current budget and project administration aspects of MOE and MRDC.

The OECD had previously addressed this issue under the project on "Supporting the Development of an Investment/Action Plan to Help Implement the New Strategy of the Government of Moldova for Water Supply and Sanitation" implemented in 2009-10 (for more detail see (OECD, 2011). Among other recommendations, the project proposed ways to improve regulation of WSS sector planning and budgeting co-ordination.

Figure 7.1 illustrates various process requirements, budgeting and reporting templates, as well as transition mechanisms, presented by the previous OECD project.

The aforementioned report has more a detailed presentation of all the stages and recommended templates. One can see that the role of the **WSS Commission**, created by government decree on 23 December 2009, is very important. Unfortunately, the actual role of the Commission is not visible; its revitalisation is strongly recommended. Another option is other similar alternative mechanisms that can make policy-level decisions and be held accountable for their implementation. Such discussion and decisions on institutional roles cannot and must not be made without considering the political economy realities. The National Policy Dialogue (NPD) is the best forum and format to discuss this issue; and putting this issue on the agenda for follow-up NPD meetings is recommended.

In any case, the review of existing procedures considers the earlier recommendations are still valid. Therefore, this project supports the earlier package and recommends the NPD revisit the earlier OECD report and decide on recommendations.

Figure 7.1 also illustrates the regulation of information formats during investment. This issue is relevant to the next area for improvements in current arrangements, discussed next.

Improving regional planning, performance-based planning and monitoring and evaluation systems

It was indicated earlier in the report that types and attributes of information by various actors (MOE and MRDC) varied in standards, project parameters and planning-budgeting-monitoring-reporting requirements. Separate decision-making processes on individual projects may be unavoidable; the country carries detached information flows at the sector level as an additional implicit cost as overlaps and omissions may occur.

Figure 7.1. **Co-ordination of information flows in WSS sector budget formulation process**

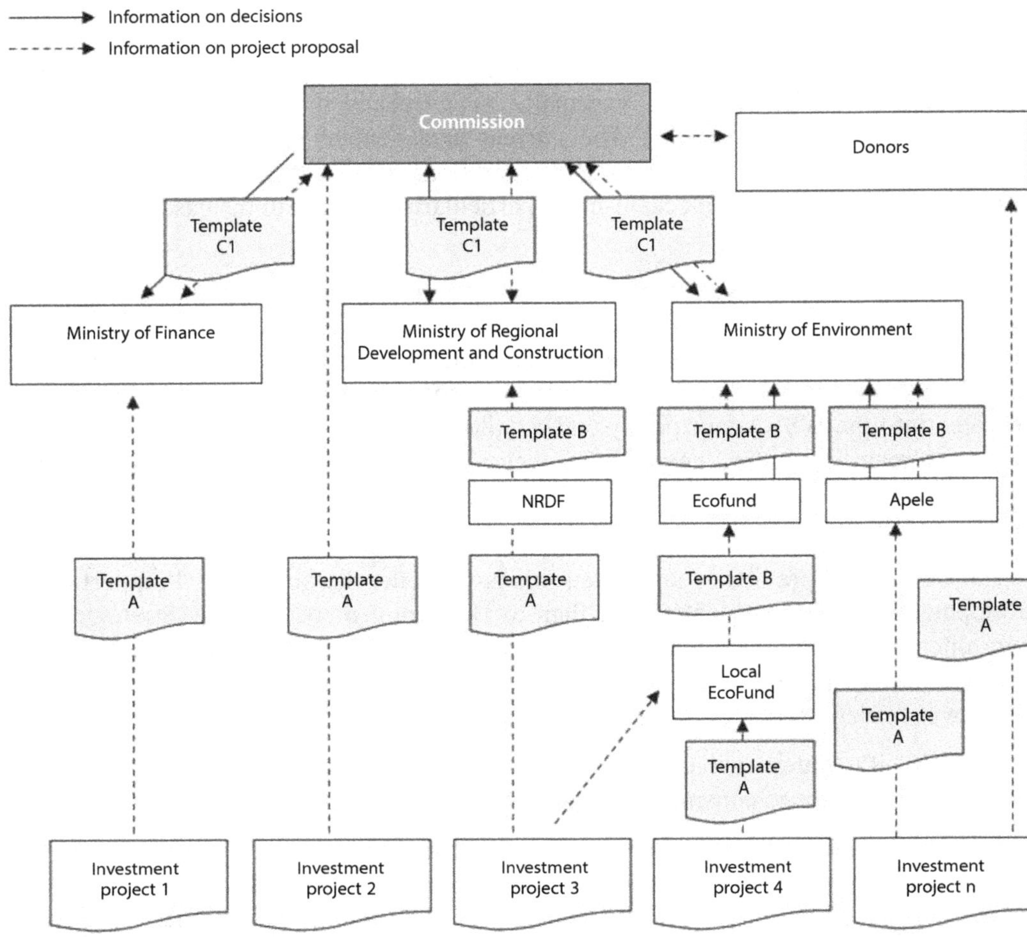

Source: quoted from the 2011 OECD report "Supporting the Development of a Mid-Term Action and Investment Plan for WSS in Moldova", which was submitted as a set of PDF documents to the Ministry of Environment of Moldova. The project documents are available upon request.

Therefore, there are two distinct areas for improvement in information flows:

- MRDC must lead a process of improving the regional planning system so that the rayon-level development plans (including aspects on WSS systems) are regularly updated. MRDC will also aggregate the bottom-up rayon development plans with the top-down policy directions. Most importantly, however, MRDC will ensure those plans inform project decisions both within MRDC and MOE. To that end, given the political economy environment, regional planning information should be incorporated into the overall WSS budget decision-making system, as per Figure 7.1.
- MRDC employs project investment-related templates that incorporate a more elaborate set of performance indicators than the one used by MOE. However, both ministries have not employed the templates and information requirement standards recommended by the earlier OECD project. This is unfortunate as these standards could be employed effectively in the WSS system in Moldova. Performance-informed budget decision making is important both at sector and individual project-level decision making. Therefore, we recommend to review and adopt a standard

set of project information requirements to be used by both MRDC and MOE. Moreover, we would also advise relevant government authorities to invite donors to use the same templates as well. Standardisation of information requirements will bring noticeable benefits in a very short time. It will also allow creation of a database that will meet the needs of MOE, MRDC and donors, and help streamline requirements.

Modernising infrastructure construction and design standards

It is beyond the scope of this study to come up with specific and detailed technical parameters of construction and design standards. However, the study observes the need to modernise the whole system in relation to the WSS sector by incorporating the new economic and demographic realities into the standards. The shift to a more liberal and market-oriented economy, high labour migration and recent demographic trends in Moldova inevitably influenced the pattern and nature of consumer behaviour in water consumption. The announced tariff policy will further change patterns as water consumption has some price elasticity and higher tariffs will drive consumption rates even lower. Soviet-era standards and norms for water consumption are now far from the actual consumption pattern and demand for water. Ignorance of those changes transforms into higher costs of project implementation.

Therefore, the study recommends addressing this issue and co-operating with relevant public organisations on finding interim and/or final solutions to this aspect, at least in the WSS infrastructure design and construction sectors.

7.5. Scenarios

The study outlined four scenarios reflecting possible development of policy approaches:

- No policy intervention
- All cards on water supply
- Framework for decentralised social measures
- Centralised WSS social measures.

Elaboration of social support measures is required as part of the improved domestic financial support mechanisms for WSS sector.

The policy of leaving things as they are is not viable over the longer term. Therefore, scenario A could not be recommended.

It is a country's political choice to adopt a more centralised or more decentralised approach. In Moldova, conditions for a centralised approach to social measures are not that favourable. On the other hand, this study is sceptical about the potential impact of decentralised solutions; leaving social aspects to local government will not yield much benefit to those who need it most.

Implementing smart social measures is therefore an economical, organisational and political challenge. If Moldova is ready, the study would recommend Scenario D, taking into account lessons learned from Armenia. It could lead, for instance, to the targeted rebate scheme elaborated in Annex E. It may even leave room for local customisation, if preferred.

Implementing a more coherent policy package requires the appropriate political economy environment, i.e. political will, technical assistance and a determination to overcome resistance and legal obstacles. Local government is constitutionally competent to manage water supply and related social affairs.

If, however, the conditions for successful policy intervention are not in place, then it would be better to follow the example of Romania and focus on water supply, cost recovery, investment and external finance. These will ultimately also improve the situation of vulnerable groups. In any case, there is no point in wasting resources on schemes that fail to specifically target lower income groups.

7.6. Road map for enhancement of domestic financial support mechanisms

The following roadmap is therefore recommended:

- Agree on the current situation.
- Distinguish between temporary fixes and structural solutions.
- Formulate realistic scenarios reflecting real developments and reliable forecasts.
- Agree on which scenario would be optimal.
- Define and implement policy actions, including risk mitigation measures.

The first step has been achieving consensus on the current situation. The second step would then be to act.

Systematically improving access to drinking water is a good structural social measure because it's an investment rather than a subsidy of some kind.

Tariff-related measures cannot be categorised so easily. Water conservation programmes provide a structural solution. This cannot be said about the reduced extent of full cost recovery. Over the long term, it rather aggravates the social problem.

In the context of EU accession and on the grounds of economic efficiency, cross-subsidies other than among types of households have had their day. They will eventually be phased out and can only be part of a transitional solution/temporary fix.

Tariff structures may be set up to provide a long-term, targeted pro-poor solution. Too often, however, tariff structures miss their goal. Rebates and voucher systems with their inherent flexibility look promising either as temporary or permanent social measures.

Income support measures also fall short. For some of these measures, a more elaborate social security system is needed, but this may take time to develop. The traditional welfare state facilities of Western Europe may not be achievable, affordable or perhaps even desirable. Targeted, pragmatic hardship support at the local level is welcome, but it is not part of structural solution for a country where perhaps 20% of the population faces hardship.

Overall, the study recommends sticking to the suggested sequence in policy making. Considering the project has already taken steps 1 and 2, the National Policy Dialogue can take the next step. This involves agreeing on a scenario for Moldova that it is determined to implement.

As discussed above, the choice for a particular scenario is far from easy. One would ideally opt for Scenario D, i.e. centralised social measures. If it is possible to overcome implementation risks and uncertainty, then the population can benefit from a number of additional social measures compared to Scenario B. These social measures are in addition to a strong focus on improving infrastructure that should be part of national policy anyway. If the choice is Scenario D, then Annex E provides a SMART policy measure that can be implemented.

References

AMAC (Association of Moldova Apacanals) database, http://www.amac.md.

BOOST database, http://wbi.worldbank.org/boost/boost-initiative.

Further reading

AST and GDN (2013), *Policy alternatives in subsidizing the water sector in Armenia, Policy Brief*, Advanced Social Technologies and Global Development Network, Washington, DC, http://gdn.int/admin/uploads/editor/files/GDNPolicyBrief_AST.pdf.

Barraqué, Bernard and Cédric Le Bris (2007), *Water Sector Regulation in France*, CESifo DICE Report 5 (2), 2007, 4-12, https://www.cesifo-group.de/ifoHome/publications/docbase/details.html?docId=14567363.

European Environment Agency (2013), *Assessment of cost recovery through water pricing*, EEA *Technical Report,* No. 16/2013, Copenhagen.

European Union (2009), *European Cohesion Policy in Romania*, Brussels, http://ec.europa.eu/regional_policy/sources/docgener/informat/country2009/ro_en.pdf.

Government of Moldova, *National Environmental Fund Reports, 2012-14.*

Government of Moldova (2014), WSS Strategy for 2014-28, http://lex.justice.md/ru/352311/.

Government of Moldova (2013), *Report of the National Bureau of Statistics and the National Centre for Public Health*, Government of Moldova, Budget calendar.

Government of Moldova (2013), *Ministry of Environment Annual Report.*

Government of Moldova (2012), Operational Manual on using funds from NFRD approved by Decision No. 4/12 dated 23 February 2012.

IBNET (2014), *The IBNET Water Supply and Sanitation Blue Book 2014*, The International, Benchmarking Network for Water and Sanitation Utilities Databook/World Bank, Washington, DC.

IMF (2013), *Republic of Moldova poverty reduction strategy paper – joint staff advisory note*, International Monetary Fund *Country Report,* No. 13/270, Washington, DC.

Komives, K. et al. (2005), *Water, Electricity, and the Poor: Who Benefits from Utility Subsidies?,* World Bank, Washington, DC.

Mascarau, G. (2008), *Le service public d'assainissement non collectif*, http://slideplayer.fr/slide/177257/.

NBS (2014), *Aspects of the standard of living of population in 2013*, Results of the household budget survey, National Bureau of Statistics of the Republic of Moldova, Chisinau.

Nauges C. and D. Wittington (2010), *Estimation of water demand in developing countries: An Overview*, *World Bank Research Observer*, Vol. 25/2, Washington, DC.

OECD (2010), *Pricing Water Resources and Sanitation Services*, OECD Publishing, Paris.

OECD (2002), *Social Issues in the Provision and Pricing of Water Services*, OECD Publishing, Paris.

OECD EAP Task Force (2007), *Implementation of a national finance strategy for the water supply and sanitation sector in Armenia, advising the Armenian water authorities on the design and monitoring of a sound tariff policy (Task 3)*, OECD Publishing, Paris.

Popa, T. (2014), *A smart mechanism for financing water and infrastructure*, *Water Utility Management International*, March 2014, pp. 5-9, London.

Poghosyan, S. (2014), *Measuring benefit incidence for water subsidization program in Armenia*, presentation at the methodological conference on measuring social inequality in the South Caucasus and its neighbourhood, Yerevan, 2014.

Smets, H. (2002), *Social protection in urban water sector in OECD countries*, presentation at an expert workshop, Paris, 4-5 March 2002.

Strosser, P. (2011), *Economic instruments for 'better' water management and application, food for thought from Armenia and elsewhere*, presentation at EU WI Eastern Europe, Caucasus and Central Asia workshop, Bucharest, 7-8 November 2011.

Ukrainian Pilot Project Team of the UNECE (2013), *Assessing progress in achieving equitable access to water and sanitation, pilot project in Ukraine*, *Country Report*, United Nations Economic Commission for Europe, www.unece.org/fileadmin/DAM/env/water/activities/Equitable_access/Country_report__Pilot_project_Ukraine_rev.pdf.

UNDP (2013), *The third national report on Millennium Development Goals in Moldova: Progress achieved, remaining issues and future options*, 24 September 2013, United Nations Development Programme, www.md.undp.org/content/moldova/en/home/presscenter/pressreleases/.

UNICEF and WHO (2012), *Progress on Drinking Water and Sanitation: 2012 Update*, Joint Monitoring Programme for Water Supply and Sanitation, United Nations Children's Fund, New York; World Health Organization, Geneva, www.unicef.org/media/files/JMPreport2012.pdf.

Verbeeck, G. and B. Vucijak (2014), *Towards effective social measures in WSS*, presentation at the conference on regional water utility management, Tirana, 5-7 November 2014, http://balkansjointconference.org/wp-content/uploads/2014/11/Giel-Verbeeck-Towards-effective-social-measures-in-WSS..pdf.

World Bank (2014), *Enhanced social safety nets for Moldova's poorest households*, www.worldbank.org/en/results/2014/04/15/enhanced-social-safety-nets-for-moldovas-poorest-households.

World Bank (2013), *Water sector regionalisation review*, Republic of Moldova, World Bank, Washington, DC.

WB (World Bank) & IAWD (International Association of Water Supply Companies in the Danube River Catchment Area), (2009), *Danube Water Program*, World Bank, Washington, DC; International Association of Water Supply Companies in the Danube River Catchment Area, Vienna, World Bank and Inter-American Development Bank, www.danube-water-program.org/media/DWP_brochure-MAIL_0914.pdf.

World Development Indicators (WDI) database, World Bank, http://databank.worldbank.org/data/reports.aspx?source=world-development-indicators.

Zetland, D. (2014), *Living with Water Scarcity*, Aquanomics Press, Amsterdam.

Annex A

IBNET data on water supply and sanitation performance in Moldova and reference countries

Table A.1. **INBET Indicator/Country: Moldova**

Latest year available	2010	2011	2012
Surface area (km²)	33 846	33 846	33 846
GNI per capita, Atlas method (current USD)	1 820	1 980	2 070
Total population (thousands)	3 562	3 559	3 555
Urban population (%)	47	48	49
Total urban population (thousands)	1 672	1 696	1 747
MDGs			
Access to improved water sources 2010 (%)	99	99	99
Access to improved sanitation 2010 (%)	89	89	89
IBNET sourced data			
Number of utilities reporting in IBNET sample	39	39	39
Population served (water), (thousands)	1 171	1 182	1 184
Size of the sample: Total population living in service area (water supply), (thousands)	1 467	1 438	1 420
Services coverage			
Water coverage (%)	80	83	84
Sewerage coverage (%)	67	69	70
Operational efficiency			
Electrical energy costs vs. operating costs (%) (share of energy cost as % of operational expenses)	25	24	24
Nonrevenue water (%)	45.00	44.00	44.00
Nonrevenue water (m³/km/day)	32	29	30
Staff W/1 000 W population served (W/1 000 W population served)	2.50	2.30	2.30
Continuity of service (hrs/day) (duration of water supply, hours)	20.30	20.80	21.30
Financial efficiency			
Water sold that is metered (%)	85	85	90
Collection period (days)	246	273	282
Collection ratio (%)	98	97	101
Average revenue W & WW (USD/m³ water sold)	1.06	1.15	1.14
Operational cost W & WW (USD/m³ water sold)	0.93	1.07	1.05
Operating cost coverage (ratio)	1.14	1.08	1.09
Production and consumption			
Water production (l/person/day)	248.00	236.00	240.00
Total water consumption (l/person/day)	137.00	133.00	133.00
Residential consumption (l/person/day)	106	103	103
Poverty and affordability			
Total revenues/service population/GNI (% GNI per capita) (average revenues)	2.91	2.82	2.67
Annual bill for households consuming 6 m³ of water/month (USD/yr)	94.11	103.87	110.85
Ratio of industrial to residential tariff (level of cross-subsidy)	3.44	3.53	3.43

Note: **W**: (potable) water supply; **WW**: (domestic) wastewater collection and treatment.

Source: IBNET data (database of the World Bank), www.IBNET.org, based on UNICEF and WHO (2012), *Progress on Drinking Water and Sanitation: 2012 Update*, https://www.unicef.org/media/files/JMPreport2012.pdf.

Table A.2. **INBET Indicator/Country: Armenia**

Latest year available	2008	2009	2010
Surface area (km²)	29 743	29 743	29 743
GNI per capita, Atlas method (current USD)	3 340	3 440	3 330
Total population (thousands)	3 079	3 085	3 092
Urban population (%)	64	64	64
Total urban population (thousands)	1 974	1 977	1 981
MDGs			
Access to improved water sources 2010 (%)	98	98	98
Access to improved sanitation 2010 (%)	90	90	90
IBNET sourced data			
Number of utilities reporting in IBNET sample	5	5	5
Population served (water), (thousands)	1 752	1 976	2 000
Size of the sample: Total population living in service area (water supply), (thousands)	2 177	2 187	2 188
Services coverage			
Water coverage (%)	80	90	91
Sewerage coverage (%)	35	37	37
Operational efficiency			
Electrical energy costs vs. operating costs (%) (share of energy cost as % of operational expenses)	21	20	16
Nonrevenue water (%)	84.00	84.00	83.00
Nonrevenue water (m³/km/day)	95	109	102
Staff W/1 000 W population served (W/1 000 W population served)	1.60	1.60	1.50
Continuity of service (hrs/day) (duration of water supply, hours)	13.20	14.00	15.20
Financial efficiency			
Water sold that is metered (%)	78	83	91
Collection period (days)	266	296	281
Collection ratio (%)	87	79	80
Average revenue W & WW (USD/m³ water sold)	0.47	0.44	0.47
Operational cost W & WW (USD/m³ water sold)	0.44	0.45	0.47
Operating cost coverage (ratio)	1.05	0.98	0.98
Production and consumption			
Water production (l/person/day)	936.00	812.00	759.00
Total water consumption (l/person/day)	151.00	128.00	126.00
Residential consumption (l/person/day)	94	85	83
Poverty and affordability			
Total revenues/service population/GNI (% GNI per capita) (average revenues)	0.78	0.60	0.65
Annual bill for households consuming 6 m³ of water/month (USD/yr)	32.10	29.74	35.86
Ratio of industrial to residential tariff (level of cross-subsidy)	1.46	1.45	1.39

Note: **W**: (potable) water supply; **WW**: (domestic) wastewater collection and treatment.

Source: IBNET data (database of the World Bank), www.IBNET.org, based on UNICEF and WHO (2012), *Progress on Drinking Water and Sanitation: 2012 Update*, https://www.unicef.org/media/files/JMPreport2012.pdf.

Table A.3. **INBET Indicator/Country: Romania**

Latest year available	2008	2009	2010
Surface area (km^2)	238 391	238 391	238 391
GNI per capita, Atlas method (current USD)	8 290	8 250	8 010
Total population (thousands)	21 514	21 480	21 438
Urban population (%)	53	53	53
Total urban population (thousands)	11 402	11 385	11 362
MDGs			
Access to improved water sources 2010 (%)	99	99	99
Access to improved sanitation 2010 (%)	88 (2000)	88 (2000)	88 (2000)
IBNET sourced data			
Number of utilities reporting in IBNET sample	19	20	20
Population served (water), (thousands)	3 968	4 518	4 952
Size of the sample: Total population living in service area (water supply), (thousands)	4 715	5 478	5 926
Services coverage			
Water coverage (%)	84	82	84
Sewerage coverage (%)	69	65	62
Operational efficiency			
Electrical energy costs vs. operating costs (%) (share of energy cost as % of operational expenses)	15	12	11
Nonrevenue water (%)	49.00	49.00	51.00
Nonrevenue water (m^3/km/day)	61	48	43
Staff W/1 000 W population served (W/1 000 W population served)	2.00	2.10	2.00
Continuity of service (hrs/day) (duration of water supply, hours)	24.00	24.00	24.00
Financial efficiency			
Water sold that is metered (%)	92	92	95
Collection period (days)	80	80	87
Collection ratio (%)	107	108	112
Average revenue W & WW (USD/m^3 water sold)	1.20	1.08	1.02
Operational cost W & WW (USD/m^3 water sold)	1.12	0.98	0.94
Operating cost coverage (ratio)	1.07	1.10	1.08
Production and consumption			
Water production (l/person/day)	371.00	336.00	311.00
Total water consumption (l/person/day)	191.00	172.00	153.00
Residential consumption (l/person/day)	111	106	103
Poverty and affordability			
Total revenues/service population/GNI (% GNI per capita) (average revenues)	1.01	0.82	0.71
Annual bill for households consuming 6 m^3 of water/month (USD/yr)	129.34	98.51	82.27
Ratio of industrial to residential tariff (level of cross-subsidy)	1.37	1.40	1.51

Note: **W**: (potable) water supply; **WW**: (domestic) wastewater collection and treatment.

Source: IBNET data (database of the World Bank), www.IBNET.org, based on UNICEF and WHO (2012), *Progress on Drinking Water and Sanitation: 2012 Update*, https://www.unicef.org/media/files/JMPreport2012.pdf.

Table A.4. **INBET Indicator/Country: Russian Federation**

Latest year available	2008	2009	2010
Surface area (km²)	17 098 242	17 098 242	17 098 242
GNI per capita, Atlas method (current USD)	9 290	10 000	10 810
Total population (thousands)	141 910	142 389	142 960
Urban population (%)	74	74	74
Total urban population (thousands)	105 013	105 368	105 790
MDGs			
Access to improved water sources 2010 (%)	97	97	97
Access to improved sanitation 2010 (%)	70	70	70
IBNET sourced data			
Number of utilities reporting in IBNET sample	82	95	80
Population served (water), (thousands)	43 164	45 306	54 837
Size of the sample: Total population living in service area (water supply), (thousands)	42 070	45 249	54 837
Services coverage			
Water coverage (%)	100	100	100
Sewerage coverage (%)	94	94	95
Operational efficiency			
Electrical energy costs vs. operating costs (%) (share of energy cost as % of operational expenses)	18	25	22
Nonrevenue water (%)	21.00	24.00	23.00
Nonrevenue water (m³/km/day)	56	60	54
Staff W/1 000 W population served (W/1 000 W population served)	1.40	1.30	1.30
Continuity of service (hrs/day) (duration of water supply, hours)	24.00	24.00	24.00
Financial efficiency			
Water sold that is metered (%)	—	74	—
Collection period (days)	92	95	99
Collection ratio (%)	91	92	88
Average revenue W & WW (USD/m³ water sold)	0.63	0.73	0.85
Operational cost W & WW (USD/m³ water sold)	0.45	0.52	0.60
Operating cost coverage (ratio)	1.40	1.40	1.41
Production and consumption			
Water production (l/person/day)	436.00	415.00	384.00
Total water consumption (l/person/day)	343.00	316.00	296.00
Residential consumption (l/person/day)	216	199	182
Poverty and affordability			
Total revenues/service population/GNI (% GNI per capita) (average revenues)	0.85	0.84	0.85
Annual bill for households consuming 6 m³ of water/month (USD/yr)	27.83	32.17	37.64
Ratio of industrial to residential tariff (level of cross-subsidy)	1.45	1.27	1.24

Note: **W**: (potable) water supply; **WW**: (domestic) wastewater collection and treatment.

Source: IBNET data (database of the World Bank), www.IBNET.org, based on UNICEF and WHO (2012), *Progress on Drinking Water and Sanitation: 2012 Update*, https://www.unicef.org/media/files/JMPreport2012.pdf.

Table A.5. **INBET Indicator/Country: Ukraine**

Latest year available	2008	2009	2010
Surface area (km²)	603 500	603 500	603 500
GNI per capita, Atlas method (current USD)	1 540	1 950	2 570
Total population (thousands)	47 105	46 788	46 509
Urban population (%)	68	68	68
Total urban population (thousands)	31 937	31 750	31 589
MDGs			
Access to improved water sources 2010 (%)	98	98	98
Access to improved sanitation 2010 (%)	94	94	94
IBNET sourced data			
Number of utilities reporting in IBNET sample	16	16	16
Population served (water), (thousands)	2 703	2 721	2 736
Size of the sample: Total population living in service area (water supply), (thousands)	3 452	3 432	3 411
Services coverage			
Water coverage (%)	78	79	80
Sewerage coverage (%)	63	64	67
Operational efficiency			
Electrical energy costs vs. operating costs (%) (share of energy cost as % of operational expenses)	30	33	36
Nonrevenue water (%)	45.00	44.00	45.00
Nonrevenue water (m³/km/day)	77	77	75
Staff W/1 000 W population served (W/1 000 W population served)	2.20	2.10	2.10
Continuity of service (hrs/day) (duration of water supply, hours)	22.00	22.00	22.00
Financial efficiency			
Water sold that is metered (%)	27	31	36
Collection period (days)	278	251	225
Collection ratio (%)	92	84	92
Average revenue W & WW (USD/m³ water sold)	0.25	0.32	0.44
Operational cost W & WW (USD/m³ water sold)	0.30	0.37	0.48
Operating cost coverage (ratio)	0.84	0.87	0.91
Production and consumption			
Water production (l/person/day)	496.36	494.64	480.00
Total water consumption (l/person/day)	273.00	277.00	264.00
Residential consumption (l/person/day)	231	224	208
Poverty and affordability			
Total revenues/service population/GNI (% GNI per capita) (average revenues)	1.62	1.66	1.65
Annual bill for households consuming 6 m³ of water/month (USD/yr)	18.07	29.49	37.32
Ratio of industrial to residential tariff (level of cross-subsidy)	5.30	4.93	3.25

Note: **W**: (potable) water supply; **WW**: (domestic) wastewater collection and treatment.

Source: IBNET data (database of the World Bank), www.IBNET.org, based on UNICEF and WHO (2012), *Progress on Drinking Water and Sanitation: 2012 Update*, https://www.unicef.org/media/files/JMPreport2012.pdf.

Reference

UNICEF and WHO (2012), *Progress on Drinking Water and Sanitation: 2012 Update*, United Nations Children's Fund, New York, and World Health Organization, Geneva, https://www.unicef.org/media/files/JMPreport2012.pdf.

Annex B

Financial flows and performance of selected Apacanals in 2013

in MDL thousands

	Chisinau	Calaras	Leova	Orhei	Balti	Floresti	Anenii	Soroca	Ceadr-Lunga	Stefan-Voda	Straseni	Amen-Ver	TOTAL
Share of non-revenue water (**NRW**) in the service area	35%	53%	35%	43%	44%	50%	53%	40%	40%	30%	60%	21%	42%
Water supply													
Bills to households	283 407	3 137	1 826	8 662	28 259	4 813	2 929	6 403	3 795	1 601	2 482	3 406	**350 722**
Bills actually paid by households	241 833	2 977	1 725	8 620	28 447	4 784	2 924	6 208	3 393	1 757	2 537	2 592	**307 796**
Bills to organisations/businesses	141 675	1 281	889	2 813	30 718	2 419	899	6 730	1 435	711	651	1 370	**191 591**
Bills actually paid by organisations/businesses	138 479	1 622	926	3 539	31 263	2 412	827	6 821	1 211	779	631	1 117	**189 626**
Sanitation													
Bills to households	36 216	956	1 300	2 014	8 150	624	1 020	512	1 248			779	**52 819**
Bills actually paid by households	30 904	1 001	357	2 004	8 179	620	1 016	496	1 679			645	**46 900**
Bills to organisations/businesses	114 158	1 235	688	6 041	20 271	3 285	1 392	2 010	2 125			2 036	**153 241**
Bills actually paid by organisations/businesses	111 583	1 559	687	7 600	20 569	3 269	1 318	2 037	1 651			1 515	**151 789**
Financial performance													
Sales	579 923	8 910	5 543	20 077	79 126	15 774	6 582	14 002	8 560	4 800	5 254	11 900	**760 451**
Cost of sales	405 848	4 383	4 209	15 453	75 519	13 502	5 896	11 058	6 954	3 691	4 076	10 080	**560 668**
Gross profit	174 075	4 527	1 334	4 624	3 607	2 272	687	2 945	1 606	1 109	1 178	1 820	**199 783**
Other income (specify)	8 453	316	0.3	1 620	2 020	163	126	448	390	55	129	1 095	**14 815**
Distribution costs	147 737	58		1 416	2 946		87	48			460	-	**152 752**
Administrative expenses	81 239	1 932	861	3 144	10 054	3 237	1 230	1 791	1 634	1 815	1 041	1 714	**109 690**
Other expenses	19 056	2 121	-	650	1 911	204	16	669	158	270	161	165	**25 382**
Finance costs and costs of other economic activities	3 150	292	174	(378)	8 014	2 993		2 315	79	928	(282)	87	**17 371**
Profit before tax	(68 654)	441	300	1 412	(17 298)	3 997)	(521)	(1 430)	124	(1 849)	(73)	950	**(90 597)**
Income tax expense	5 443	15	17	439								138	**6 052**
Profit for the year	**(74 097)**	**427**	**282**	**972**	**(17 298)**	**3 997)**	**(521)**	**(1 430)**	**124**	**(1 849)**	**(73)**	**812**	**(96 649)**

Note: Data for Stefan-Voda and Straseni include both water supply and sanitation.

Source: Authors' findings based on feedback obtained from the Apacanals survey held as part of the project.

Annex C

Survey of stakeholders' perceptions regarding social support systems

Categories of questions

A. Questions on supply-related social measures
B. Questions on tariff-related measures
C. Questions on income support

Colouring

■ Responses from urban operators, simple average of 15 respondents

░ Response from municipal enterprises, simple average of 5 respondents

Meaning of the scale

0. I totally disagree; **1**. I strongly disagree; **2**. I disagree; **3**. I somewhat disagree; **4**. I faintly disagree;
5. Neutral/no opinion; **6**. I faintly agree; **7**. I somewhat agree; **8**. I agree; **9**. I strongly agree; **10**. I totally agree.

Perceptions and values: To what extent do you agree with the following statements?

			0	1	2	3	4	5	6	7	8	9	10
1	A	The Eco Fund should focus on its social function of providing access for the poor.						■			░		
2	A	The Fund for Regional Development (NFRD) should focus on providing access for the poor.								■	░		
3	B	The economic regulator (ANRE) should consider the affordability (social aspects) of tariffs.								■	░		
4	B	The economic regulator (ANRE) should instruct social policies for identified poor households, such as forbidding disconnection						■		░			
5	B	The economic regulator (ANRE) should determine a tariff mechanism that favours poorer households.								■ ░			
6	A	Local investment subsidies focus on access to drinking water for lower income groups.								■ ░			
7	B	Local operating subsidies for service providers are essential for social cases in the service area.						░	■				
8	B	Local operational subsidies are essential for keeping tariffs affordable.							■	░			
9	B	There is need for a tariff system that lowers the price of the first, most essential cubic metres per month.							■ ░				
10	B	In the service area, the existing billing system (hardware, software and personnel) cannot deal with a more complex billing system than the current one.					■		░				

			0	1	2	3	4	5	6	7	8	9	10
11	A	Standpipes are a good alternative for those who cannot afford paying for running water at home.											
12	A	Providing access to piped drinking water is much more important than supporting poor households that have access already.											
13	C	In the service area, there is no disconnection of households for those who truly cannot afford paying the service.											
14	C	In the service area, the vast majority of social cases have been identified.											
15	C	The fee collector has the skills and autonomy to deal with customers that cannot afford paying the bill.											
16	B	A social tariff system could easily be agreed as part of a service agreement between operator and municipality.											
17		Municipality is actively supporting the service provider (through cadastral information, police support or otherwise).											
18	B	Water operators know themselves best how to deal with poor customers by offering payment delay, instalments or otherwise.											
19		Only a regional operator has the capacity to implement a social tariff policy.											
20		Customers understand that they need in one way or another to pay a bit more for their water in order to support poorer households.											

Cross-subsidies: To what extent do you agree with the following statements?

		0	1	2	3	4	5	6	7	8	9	10
1	Other municipal services cross subsidise water and sanitation services in the service area											
2	Water and sanitation services cross subsidise other municipal services.											
3	There cannot be cross subsidy because services in the service area are separated, either legally or physically.											
4	Households pay less for water than industry and businesses per cubic metre in this service area.	Less than 50%			Less than 30%			Less than 10%		No difference		

Sources: Authors' findings based on feedback obtained from the Apacanals survey held as part of the project.

Annex D

Social aspects of ANRE 2015 tariff methodology

The National Agency for Regulation in Energy, ANRE, published the new tariff methodology on 13 February 2015, http://lex.justice.md/index.php?action=view&view=doc&lang=1&id=356819.

At the time of finalising this report, an official English version of the new tariff methodology was not yet available. A number of comments are provided below with respect to the social aspects of the methodology based also on comments and interviews with local experts.

The positive elements in the methodology are:

1. Focus on cost recovery

   The new tariff methodology has a very outspoken focus on the recovery of both operational and capital costs. This will help operators to realise network extension plans and to extend services. This ultimately will benefit particularly lower income groups as they typically live in more peripheral areas that do not have full service.

2. Costs incurred for non-water services are not eligible for tariff calculation; this protects the population at large and is (also) in the interest of socially vulnerable groups.

3. The structure only allows a single volumetric tariff. This tariff structure avoids smaller and possibly poorer customers paying a higher price per cubic metre than large customers. On the other hand, it does not foresee the possibility of introducing block tariffs. However, as was noted above, block tariffs are not a very efficient social measure.

4. Affordability has been defined, namely as 5% of average income.

There are also a number of concerns.

1. The methodology does not provide for any (even temporary) form of a cross subsidy.

   Household tariffs are kept low mostly through a cross subsidy from businesses to households through a difference in tariffs. The new methodology does not foresee any such difference. While this is in line with economic efficiency and EU principles, there is no transition period planned to phase out tariff differentials. This can lead to (unnecessarily) drastic increases in tariffs for households. A transition period of four-five years would ease the process.

2. The methodology does not provide for any form of social tariff or measure.

Any form of social support associated in the water sector must come from municipalities in the form of income support. As outlined in Chapter 4, this is not always efficient. A rebate system as outlined in the next Annex may not be consistent with the new methodology unless it is fully paid for by the municipality, instead of by other household consumers.

A number of other publications are available on the ANRE website. At the time of writing this report, some were still published only for consultation.

- Methodology for tariffs on auxiliary services (published for consultation 4 March 2015)

  http://anre.md/files/Acte%20Normative/cons%20publice/Proiect%20Metodologie%20servicii%20auxiliare%200303%202015%20V1.doc

- Regulation on water and sewerage service (published for consultation 17 November 2014)

  http://anre.md/files/Acte%20Normative/cons%20publice/Proiect%20Regulament%20serviciul%20public%20apa%20canalizare%20Fin.doc

- Regulation on the quality indicators for water and sewerage service (still to be published)

- Regulation on procurements (published for consultation 22 October 2014)

  http://anre.md/files/proiect_legislativ/Proiect%20Regulament%20achizi%C5%A3ii%20Final%2020%2001.doc

- Regulation on the establishment and approval for purposes of determining tariffs, technological consumption and water losses in public water supply systems (still to be published)

Annex E

Elaborated example of a rebate system in tariff methodology

There are many social measures possible in water supply and sanitation (WSS): the challenge is to apply them in a SMART manner:

1. Specific

   What is exactly the measure and who carries it out?

2. Measurable

   How many resources are used for the measure and to what extent do they arrive where they should?

3. Attainable

   Is the measure adequate for the associated target?

4. Realistic

   Can it be expected that stakeholders will understand, apply and obey the measure?

5. Time-bound

   When is the measure going to be implemented?

A SMART rebate system is elaborated below. It is presented as an illustration rather than as the only possible approach.

Outline of SMART Rebate system

The rebate system intends to support low-income customers by providing a lump sum discount on the WSS bill. It has been chosen because it:

- may be designed to target low-income groups more specifically than its alternatives (in particular Increasing Block Tariffs)
- may be designed to leave room for local customisation
- is relatively simple to administer
- has a high degree of flexibility so it can be adjusted or abolished over time
- gives incentives for customers to pay bills on time
- may be designed so it does not affect the ability of the Apacanal to recover its costs.

It is called the rebate system because it provides a lump sum discount for some or all household customers i.e. between 0% and 100% of households may be made eligible for the system.

The rebate system does not change the average value of the household bill because it is an internal subsidy from households to households. It is paid for by households that are better off. The decision on the design of the rebate system stands apart from the affordability percentage. If tariffs are unaffordable for the population at large, the rebate system cannot solve that. If tariffs are unaffordable for a part of the population, the rebate system can address that, but only insofar as other customers can be obliged to compensate for the discount provided to the eligible group.

Therefore, the Apacanal will not be worse because of the rebate system. On the contrary, it may lead to a better payment discipline because the rebate can be realised only upon payment of the bill. To the extent that rebates cannot be fully realised, they even provide extra revenue to the service provider. First, rebates cannot be realised in case of late payment i.e. the rebate expires. Second, by definition, the rebate cannot lead to negative income for the Apacanal provider on a particular bill. If someone's bill is lower than the size of the rebate, then one can realise only up to the amount of the bill. The rebate may be realised only against the pure revenue of the service provider. Other taxes and charges remain payable. Because such taxes and charges may be levied on top of the revenues of the service provider, a complication may occur. However, since a discount for rapid payment is widely used in other sectors of the economy, it is expected that fiscal authorities can accept this instrument.

First, the percentage of redistribution for the Apacanal must be decided. This discretion may be left to the Apacanal, to the municipality or to the Apacanal with a requirement for consultation.

The regulator should set an appropriate maximum to protect well-off customers from paying a too large part of the total household utilities water bill. Table 7.6 sets this maximum percentage at 25%. At this level, the invoiced tariff per cubic metre will get very large. This may incur political acceptability issues. Let us suppose the Apacanal wants to use 15%.

This means that:

- The revenue requirement is increased by 15%.
- The household tariff goes up by 15%.
- The resulting extra amount of revenue is distributed among customers as a discount.

The rebate is provided to 0%-100% of customers. Those customers that receive the rebate, *and* pay their water bill on time *and* consume a relatively small amount of water pay less per cubic metre than other customers. This achieves exactly the targeted effect of Increasing Block Tariffs, but more efficiently and effectively.

Apart from setting a maximum percentage for redistribution, the regulator may leave freedom to the local community to decide on the size of the rebate and conditions for eligibility. This is more a social question that can be resolved in the given framework of the rebate system (whereby individual metering is a key condition).

- Some communities may want to structure the rebate as a lifeline and make the first cubic metre of water virtually free. This requires only a small rebate percentage.
- Others want to target the instrument to a wider group of vulnerable people. This requires a higher percentage and wider eligibility.
- Yet others may want to use it as an instrument for water conservation. In that case, everyone may be eligible.

Neither the average tariff, nor the affordability criterion, nor the average value of the bill are affected through the rebate. Because of its progressive effect, the rebate will increase the number of people for whom water services are affordable. There will always be people who cannot afford water services or need additional social assistance. Through the rebate, such cases are reduced rapidly and efficiently. It is therefore a very good first step in the process of building up social WSS measures. As a result of the rebate, everyone that keeps water consumption to an absolute minimum will have a very low water bill. Table E.1 illustrates how the rebate mechanism works in a fictitious numerical example. In this case, the rebate is phased out over a number of years; communities may also opt for a permanent rebate.

If local governments are given limited discretion in setting the rebate percentage, it should be made aware of policy instruments available and about the room for local customisation:

- the percentage of projected household revenues that will be redistributed
- the eligibility criteria for a rebate.

If the rebate is made available to specific groups, local government will have to set the criteria, inform local community and take responsibility for verification.

Table E.1. **Illustrative example of a rebate calculation (not Moldova-specific)**

Rebate calculation								
Opted for rebate percentage (the amount of household Income to be redistributed)			15%	12%	9%	6%	3%	0%
A. Original (before rebate) tariff schedule approved by regulator		**current**	**2016**	**2017**	**2018**	**2019**	**2020**	**2021**
Household tariff per m³		EUR 0.85	EUR 0.91	EUR 0.96	EUR 1.02	EUR 1.08	EUR 1.13	EUR 1.19
Legal entities per m³		EUR 0.95	EUR 0.99	EUR 1.03	EUR 1.07	EUR 1.11	EUR 1.15	EUR 1.19
B. After rebate tariff schedule								
Household tariff per m³	Increased with rebate %	EUR 0.85	EUR 1.04	EUR 1.08	EUR 1.11	EUR 1.14	EUR 1.17	EUR 1.19
Legal entities per m³	Unchanged from the original tariff	EUR 0.95	EUR 0.99	EUR 1.03	EUR 1.07	EUR 1.11	EUR 1.15	EUR 1.19

Note: The extra revenues can be redistributed as rebates according to different, locally established criteria. These may include universal household entitlement, monetary value per household or household inhabitant, type of dwelling (household, apartment).

Source: Authors' findings.

ORGANISATION FOR ECONOMIC CO-OPERATION AND DEVELOPMENT

The OECD is a unique forum where governments work together to address the economic, social and environmental challenges of globalisation. The OECD is also at the forefront of efforts to understand and to help governments respond to new developments and concerns, such as corporate governance, the information economy and the challenges of an ageing population. The Organisation provides a setting where governments can compare policy experiences, seek answers to common problems, identify good practice and work to co-ordinate domestic and international policies.

The OECD member countries are: Australia, Austria, Belgium, Canada, Chile, the Czech Republic, Denmark, Estonia, Finland, France, Germany, Greece, Hungary, Iceland, Ireland, Israel, Italy, Japan, Korea, Latvia, Luxembourg, Mexico, the Netherlands, New Zealand, Norway, Poland, Portugal, the Slovak Republic, Slovenia, Spain, Sweden, Switzerland, Turkey, the United Kingdom and the United States. The European Union takes part in the work of the OECD.

OECD Publishing disseminates widely the results of the Organisation's statistics gathering and research on economic, social and environmental issues, as well as the conventions, guidelines and standards agreed by its members.

OECD PUBLISHING, 2, rue André-Pascal, 75775 PARIS CEDEX 16
(97 2016 03 1 P) ISBN 978-92-64-25219-6 – 2017

www.ingramcontent.com/pod-product-compliance
Lightning Source LLC
Chambersburg PA
CBHW061219240926
51846CB00006B/1279
* 9 7 8 9 2 6 4 2 5 2 1 9 6 *